On This Day in
HOCKEY

On This Day in HOCKEY

Scholastic Canada Ltd.

Toronto New York London Auckland Sydney
Mexico City New Delhi Hong Kong Buenos Aires

Scholastic Canada Ltd.
604 King Street West, Toronto, Ontario M5V 1E1, Canada

Scholastic Inc.
557 Broadway, New York, NY 10012, USA

Scholastic Australia Pty Limited
PO Box 579, Gosford, NSW 2250, Australia

Scholastic New Zealand Limited
Private Bag 94407, Botany, Manakau 2163, New Zealand

Scholastic Children's Books
Euston House, 24 Eversholt Street, London NW1 1DB, UK

Library and Archives Canada Cataloguing in Publication

Zweig, Eric, 1963-
On this day in hockey / Eric Zweig.

ISBN 978-0-545-98591-8

1. Hockey—Miscellanea—Juvenile literature. 2. National Hockey
League—Miscellanea—Juvenile literature. I. Title.

GV847.Z84 2009   j796.962   C2009-901175-1

ISBN-10 0-545-98591-9

Text copyright © 2009 Eric Zweig.
Copyright © 2009 by Scholastic Canada Ltd.
All rights reserved.

6 5 4 3 2 1   Printed in Canada   09 10 11 12 13 14

For all the friends who ever played with us in the basement or the backyard — or who ever chased a tennis ball down the hill — in the old days on Argonne Crescent.

Introduction

There's a joke about the weather in Canada that says we get "10 months of winter and two months of bad hockey." Well, the truth is, our winters aren't as bad as that . . . and even when you can't get out and play it, you can still talk about hockey every day of the year if you want to. This book is certainly proof of that.

The biggest problem in putting this book together wasn't in trying to find something to say for every day. The biggest problem was that some days had so many things happening on them that it was hard to pick only one! Whenever possible, I tried to go with something that was the first, most, best or biggest thing that ever happened on that day. Sometimes, I would get up in the morning and add something new to the list that had just happened the night before. Other times, I'd be writing about things that happened long before I was born — sometimes, even before my parents or grandparents were born.

I had a lot of fun putting it all together. I hope you'll have fun reading it too!

Eric Zweig

January 1, 1973
Bobby Orr tied the record for most assists by a defenseman in one game by scoring six assists to lead the Boston Bruins to an 8–2 win over the Vancouver Canucks.

January 2, 1980
Gordie Howe became the first player in NHL history to play in five different decades. Howe's Hartford Whalers tied the Edmonton Oilers 2–2.

January 3, 1931
Nels Stewart scored two goals four seconds apart in the third period (8:24 and 8:28) to lead the Montreal Maroons past the Boston Bruins 5–3. (See December 15, 1995)

January 4, 2005
Team Canada beat Russia 6–1 in the gold medal game to win the World Junior Championship. It was Canada's first win at the tournament in eight years. The Canadian team featured future NHL stars Jeff Carter, Dion Phaneuf and Sidney Crosby. Alex Ovechkin and Evgeni Malkin led the Russian team.

January 5, 1910
The Montreal Canadiens played their first game in franchise history, beating the Cobalt Silver Kings 7–6 in overtime. The Canadiens were members of the National Hockey Association — forerunner to the NHL.

Junior Achievement

Sidney Crosby and Evgeni Malkin battle for the puck in the 2005 World Juniors.

Though it's officially known as the World Under-20 Championship, most Canadians know this tournament as the World Junior Championship. Today, it's a holiday tradition for many Canadian hockey fans over the Christmas season. Every year millions tune in to watch the tournament on TV.

The plan to create a World Junior Championship began in 1973. Three unofficial tournaments were held before the event truly got under way in the winter of 1976–77.

Finally, in 1981–82, the idea of a national junior team was born. There were no playoffs at the tournament back then. Eight teams took part, and each one played each of the other seven teams once. The medals were determined by the standings. That first year Canada won six of its seven games, and tied one. The team's biggest win was a 7–0 victory over the Soviet Union. Including the unofficial events, the Soviets had won the Junior title seven times in a row from 1974 to 1980. Since winning the event for the first time in 1982, Canada has won more gold medals at the World Junior Championship than any other country.

January 6, 1980

The Philadelphia Flyers beat Buffalo 4–2 for their 35th straight game without a loss. With no overtime or shootouts back then, the streak included 25 wins and 10 ties. The Flyers lost 7–1 to the Minnesota North Stars the next day.

January 7, 1981

Marcel Dionne of the Los Angeles Kings scored the fastest 1,000 points in NHL history, doing it in 740 games. Wayne Gretzky later broke the record, reaching 1,000 points in just 424 games in 1984.

January 8, 1947

Howie Meeker of the Maple Leafs set an NHL record for rookies. He scored five goals in one game to lead Toronto to a 10–4 win over Chicago.

January 9, 2004

Phoenix goalie Brian Boucher set a modern NHL record with his fifth consecutive shutout.*

January 10, 2008

The Washington Capitals signed Alex Ovechkin to a 13-year contract worth $124 million. The contract runs from the 2008–09 season through to 2020–21. Ovechkin became the first $100-million player in NHL history.

---

* Most hockey historians define the modern NHL to have started with the creation of the centre ice red line in 1943–44.

Boucher Blanks Them

S ince his NHL career began in 1999–2000, Brian Boucher has mostly been a backup goalie. Yet for a brief stretch with the Phoenix Coyotes during the 2003–04 season, Boucher was better than almost anyone in NHL history. Between December 31 and January 9, Boucher shut

out his opponents five games in a row.

The streak began with a 4–0 win over the Los Angeles Kings. After his third consecutive shutout, the hockey world began to take notice. The modern record for shutouts in a row was four, set by Canadiens goalie Bill Durnan in 1948–49. Durnan had won the Vezina Trophy as the NHL's best goalie six times in his seven-year career. Could someone like Brian Boucher really break his record?

On January 7, 2004, Boucher tied the record with a 3–0 win in Washington. Two days later, he broke it with a 2–0 win in Minnesota.

On January 11 Boucher almost made it six in a row. He allowed just one goal in a 1–1 tie with Atlanta. The goal came early in the first period and went in because of a lucky bounce off Coyotes defenseman David Tanabe.

January 11, 1983

The Oilers' Pat Hughes set an NHL record when he scored two short-handed goals in 25 seconds. Hughes' record came during a second-period scoring spree where Edmonton scored on five straight shots. They beat St. Louis 7–5.

January 12, 1986

Chicago's Denis Savard scored a goal just four seconds into the third period, tying the NHL record for the fastest goal from the start of a period.

January 13, 2006

Rookie Alex Ovechkin scored the first hat trick of his career. Ovechkin got all three goals to lead Washington over Anaheim 3–2. He capped his hat trick with the game-winning goal in overtime.

January 14, 1943

Alex Smart of the Montreal Canadiens set an NHL record when he scored three goals in his very first game.

January 15, 1968

Bill Masterton of the Minnesota North Stars died two days after injuring his head in a game. He is the only player in NHL history to die from an injury that occurred during a game. The Masterton Trophy was created in his honour.

January 16, 1905

Frank McGee scored 14 goals to lead the Ottawa "Silver Seven" to a 23–2 victory over Dawson City in a Stanley Cup challenge game.

January 17, 1962

Chicago goalie Glenn Hall played in his 500th consecutive game. The streak included every regular-season and playoff game since 1955. Hall received a new car and other gifts from the Black Hawks.

Mr. Goalie

Glenn Hall, known as "Mr. Goalie" was one of the greatest netminders in NHL history.

Hall was signed by the Detroit Red Wings in 1949, but didn't become their starting goalie until the 1955–56 season. He played every minute of all 70 games for Detroit that year and led the NHL with 12 shutouts. Hall played every minute of every game for Detroit again in 1956–57.

In the summer of 1957, Hall was traded to Chicago. He continued to play every minute of every game for the Black Hawks for the next four seasons. In 1961 Hall helped Chicago win the Stanley Cup. It was the first time they had won it since 1938.

On November 7, 1962, Hall finally took a seat on the bench. He had pinched a nerve in his back during practice, and it became too painful for him to play. Hall had started the game, but took himself out after Boston scored midway through the first period. Until then, Hall had played 502 games in a row during the regular season without missing a single minute. He had also played in 49 straight playoff games.

January 18, 1958

Boston rookie Willie O'Ree became the first black player in NHL history, as he took to the ice in Montreal. The Bruins beat the Canadiens 3–0.

January 19, 1932

Toronto's Charlie Conacher became the first player in Maple Leafs history to score five goals in one game. He led the Leafs to an 11–3 win over the New York Americans.

January 20, 1995

After a lockout wiped out three-and-a-half months of play, the 1994–95 NHL season finally began. The schedule was cut down to 48 games for every team. Still, the Stanley Cup Final didn't end until June 24 . . . the latest date in NHL history.

January 21, 1997

Defenseman Michel Petit played his first game for the Philadelphia Flyers, setting an NHL record at the time for the most teams played for. Petit ended up playing with 10 teams in his career, but the record is now 12 teams held by Mike Sillinger.

January 22, 1987

A snowstorm in New Jersey delayed the start of the game between the Devils and Flames for 106 minutes. Only 334 fans fought their way through the 38 centimetres of snow to see the game, which the Devils won 7–5.

Success Is Swede

Today there are NHL players from across Europe. However, there was a time when almost everyone in the league was Canadian. The few who weren't were usually from the United States.

In April 1963 the New York Rangers announced that they were trying to sign a Swedish player. That September, they invited Ulf Sterner to their training camp. Though there had been a few NHL players who had been born in Europe, all of them had grown up in Canada. Sterner was offered a contract, but he decided to go back to Sweden. In those days NHL players weren't allowed to play at the Olympics, and Sterner wanted to be with the Swedish team at the 1964 Winter Games.

Sterner signed with the Rangers for the 1964–65 season. He spent most of it in the minors, then decided to return to Sweden. He spent the rest of his career playing in Europe. It took another Swedish player to finally pave the way for European players in the NHL: Borje Salming joined the Toronto Maple Leafs in 1973–74 and quickly became a star.

January 31, 1920

Joe Malone of the Quebec Bulldogs set an NHL record for most goals scored in a game when he scored seven goals in a 10–6 win over the Toronto St. Pats. This record has never been broken.

February 1, 2003

Hayley Wickenheiser became the first woman to score a goal in a men's professional hockey league game. Wickenheiser was playing for HC Salamat in Finland.

February 2, 2003

Dany Heatley was named MVP at the All-Star Game after tying a record with four goals. At 22 years old, Heatley was the youngest player to score a hat trick in the All-Star Game. He was six days younger than Wayne Gretzky had been when he set the record in 1983.

February 3, 1924

Canada won the gold medal in hockey at the first Winter Olympics. The Toronto Granites beat the United States' team 6–1. (See April 26, 1920)

February 4, 1956

The Soviet Union won the gold medal in hockey for the first time, in their very first appearance at the Olympics.

Wicked Good

When Hayley Wickenheiser was young, people would tell her that girls didn't play hockey. Today many regard her as the best female hockey player in the world.

Wickenheiser started playing hockey when she was eight years old. Mostly, she played on boys' teams, and she was usually the best player. When she was 12, she played for Team Alberta at the 1991 Canada Winter Games. Even though many of the other girls in the tournament were 17, Wickenheiser scored the winning goal and was named the MVP in the gold medal game.

By the time she was 15, Wickenheiser had earned a spot on the Canadian national women's team and helped them win the 1994 Women's World Championship. She has been part of the team ever since.

After helping Canada win a gold medal at the 2002 Winter Olympics, Wickenheiser signed with a men's team in Finland. On January 11, 2003, she played her first game with HC Salamat. In her sixth game, on February 1, 2003, she became the first woman to score a goal in men's professional hockey.

February 5, 2009

Alex Ovechkin scored his 200th NHL goal in just his 296th career game. He was only the fifth player in NHL history to score 200 goals in fewer than 300 games.

February 6, 1973

Connie Madigan became the oldest rookie in NHL history when he played his first game for the St. Louis Blues. Madigan was 38 years old.

February 7, 1976

Maple Leafs captain Darryl Sittler scored six goals and four assists helping Toronto defeat Boston 11–4. Sittler's 10-point game set an NHL record for most points in a game, which has never been broken.

February 8, 1975

Minnesota North Stars goalie Pete LoPresti recorded his first career shutout. That made him and Sam LoPresti the first father and son to both record shutouts in the NHL. Sam had played for Chicago back in the 1940s.

February 9, 1966

The NHL officially announced six new expansion teams. The league would grow from six teams to 12 for the 1967–68 season.

Double Dare

Between 1918 and 1926, the NHL grew from just three teams to ten. However, the Great Depression and World War II forced some teams to shut down, and by 1942 there were just six teams left: the Toronto Maple Leafs, Montreal Canadiens, Boston Bruins, Detroit Red Wings, Chicago Black Hawks and New York Rangers, now known as "The Original Six."

There had been talk of NHL expansion as early as 1952. Soon Major League Baseball and the National Football League expanded, and in 1965 the NHL announced plans to do the same. On February 9, 1966, the NHL announced the six new teams: the Philadelphia Flyers, Pittsburgh Penguins, St. Louis Blues, Los Angeles Kings, Oakland Seals and Minnesota North Stars. Applications from Buffalo, Baltimore and Vancouver were turned down. The price for each of the new teams was $2 million.

On June 6, 1967, the NHL held an expansion draft. Each new team picked 20 players and entered the NHL for the 1967–68 season. The "Original Six" teams were all kept together in the East Division, while the six new teams played in the West. Expansion proved to be so popular that the NHL added six more teams during the 1970s.

February 10, 1993
Jeff Reese of the Calgary Flames set a record for goalies when he got three assists in a single game. Calgary clobbered San Jose 13–1.

February 11, 2009
Washington's Mike Green tied an NHL record for defensemen when he scored a goal for the seventh game in a row. Green then set a new record with eight in a row on February 14th.

February 12, 1949
Canada beat Denmark 47–0 in a World Championship game. It's the highest scoring game in the long history of the hockey World Championship.

February 13, 1972
Buffalo rookie Rick Martin scored his 38th goal of the year, tying the NHL record for most goals by a rookie. Sabres teammate Gil Perreault had set the record just one year before. Martin finished the year with 44 goals. The rookie record is now 76. (See July 3, 1970)

February 14, 1934
The NHL held a special All-Star Game to raise money for Maple Leafs star Ace Bailey. Bailey had suffered a career-ending injury in a game a few weeks earlier.

Toronto's Ace

Irvine "Ace" Bailey joined Toronto's hockey team in 1926–27 and quickly became one of the team's top stars. He led the NHL in both goals and points in 1928–29, and in 1932 helped the Leafs win their first Stanley Cup.

On December 12, 1933, Toronto played in Boston. During the second period, Boston's Eddie Shore hit Bailey from behind. At the time, players didn't wear helmets, and Bailey hit his head on the ice, suffering a fractured skull. Two operations saved his life, but he would never play hockey again.

The NHL held a special game to raise money for Bailey. The Maple Leafs played against a team of NHL All-Stars that featured Eddie Shore. Bailey didn't hold him responsible for his accident, and when he shook Shore's hand before the game, Maple Leaf Gardens erupted in cheers. Then it was announced that the Leafs were going to retire Bailey's number 6. He was the first player in NHL history to be given this honour. No Leaf was ever supposed to wear his number again, but before the 1968–69 season, Bailey asked that his number 6 be given to Ron Ellis.

February 15, 1922
Ottawa Senators star Punch Broadbent scored a goal for the 16th straight game. Broadbent's mark is still a record for the NHL's longest goal-scoring streak.

February 16, 2001
Mathieu Schneider became the first defenseman to score a goal against all 30 teams in the NHL after he scored to help Los Angeles beat Minnesota 4–0.

February 17, 1998
The United States beat Canada 3–1 to win the Olympic gold medal in women's hockey. The 1998 Winter Olympics in Nagano, Japan, marked the first time that women's hockey was a part of the Olympics.

February 18, 1918
Canadiens legend Georges Vezina recorded the first shutout in NHL history. Montreal blanked Toronto 9–0.

February 19, 1979
Mike Bossy of the New York Islanders became the fastest player to reach 100 goals in the NHL when he scored his 47th goal of the 1978–79 season. It took him just 129 games.

February 20, 1930
Clint Benedict of the Montreal Maroons became the first goalie to wear a mask in an NHL game. It would be almost 30 years before Jacques Plante would make the mask a standard piece of goalie equipment. (See November 1, 1959)

Father Knows Best

Wayne Gretzky's father, Walter, built a rink in the family's backyard so his son could practice hockey. He also gave Wayne his most useful piece of hockey advice: "Head for where the puck is going, not where it's been."

When Wayne was just 16 years old, he starred for the Sault Ste. Marie Greyhounds of the Ontario Hockey League. Phil Esposito's father, Pat, owned part of the team. When he

Gretzky celebrates a goal

first saw Wayne play, he told his son that he had just seen the player who was going to break all of Phil's scoring records. During his second season in the NHL in 1980–81, Gretzky collected 164 points to break Esposito's record of 152. During the 1981–82 season, Gretzky had his sights set on Esposito's goal-scoring record of 76. "Espo" was in the stands the night Gretzky went after the record in Buffalo. The Sabres kept Gretzky off the scoresheet until late in the third period, but he finally got his 77th goal . . . then added two more. Gretzky finished the season with an amazing 92 goals.

~~~ary 29, 1980

...Howe became the first player in NHL history to score 800
... goals. Wayne Gretzky is the only other player to have
...ched this milestone. (See March 23, 1994)

March 1, 1919

Newsy Lalonde of the Montreal Canadiens became the first player
to score five goals in an NHL playoff game. Over the years, Maurice
Richard, Darryl Sittler, Reggie Leach and Mario Lemieux have all tied
Newsy's record, but no one has ever broken it.

March 2, 1969

Phil Esposito became the first player in NHL history to score
100 points in a single season.

March 3, 1920

The Montreal Canadiens beat the Quebec Bulldogs 16–3. No team in
NHL history has ever scored more goals in a single game.

March 4, 1941

The Boston Bruins set an NHL record for most shots on goal with
83 in one game. Chicago goalie Sam LoPresti made 80 saves for the
Black Hawks, but still lost 3–2.

The Tigers Strike Out

The Hamilton Tigers joined the NHL in 1920. The owners of a new arena in the city paid $5,000 to buy the former Quebec City franchise. The Quebec Bulldogs were a dreadful 4–20–0 during the 1919–20

season. The team didn't do much better in Hamilton. They finished last in the NHL four years in a row.

By 1924–25, the Tigers had finally attracted some pretty good talent. The Tigers had never won more than nine games before, but they started the season 10–4–1. They finished with a record of 19–10–1 and wound up in first place. But when the season ended on March 9, the Hamilton players went on strike. They told their owners they wouldn't play in the playoffs unless each man got a bonus of $200. Other teams had given their players raises or bonuses. The Tigers had not, and NHL President Frank Calder refused to give them the bonus. The players still would not play, so Calder suspended them. In April the team was sold. The Hamilton Tigers became the New York Americans and Hamilton has been without an NHL team ever since.

March 10, 2008

Jarome Iginla became the leading goal-scorer in Calgary Flames history. Iginla's 41st goal of the 2007–08 season was the 365th of his career. That broke Theoren Fleury's team record of 364.

March 11, 1996

The final game was played at the Montreal Forum. The Canadiens beat the Dallas Stars 4–1. The Forum had been the Canadiens' permanent home since 1926. (See November 29, 1924)

March 12, 1966

Bobby Hull became the first player in NHL history to score more than 50 goals in one season when he scored his 51st goal to lead Chicago past the Rangers 4–2.

March 13, 1999

Ray Bourque became the Boston Bruins' all-time leader in games played. Bourque broke John Bucyk's team record of 1,436 games. He went on to play in 1,518 games with the Bruins.

March 14, 1948

Montreal's Maurice Richard scored a hat trick with three unassisted goals. The next player to match this feat was Rick Nash of Columbus — 61 years later on March 7, 2009.

March 15, 1970

Bobby Orr became the first defenseman to score 100 points in a single season. Orr finished the 1969–70 season as the NHL's top scorer with 120 points. He led the league again with 135 points in 1974–75. No other defenseman in NHL history has ever been the league's scoring leader.

Farewell to the Forum

The final game at the Montreal Forum was a memorable moment for all hockey fans. The Canadiens won the game that night, as they had at the Forum more than 1,500 times. Winning was important, but it was the closing ceremonies that everyone would remember. The Canadiens had invited all of the team's living legends back to the Forum to give the building a proper farewell. Fans gave Maurice Richard, the greatest of all Canadiens, a standing ovation that lasted for nearly 10 minutes.

For many years, there has been a motto on the wall of the Canadiens dressing room. It reads: "To you from failing hands we throw the torch; be yours to hold it high," and is from the poem "In Flanders Fields" by John McCrae. For the Canadiens, it means that each new generation of players is responsible for carrying on the team's great tradition. During the closing ceremonies, each of the team's former captains passed a flaming torch down a line. It was a fitting tribute for a team that had won the Stanley Cup 22 times while the Forum was their home. No NHL team has ever enjoyed so much success.

March 16, 1961

The Montreal Canadiens' Bernie "Boom Boom" Geoffrion became the second player in NHL history to score 50 goals in a season. He reached the milestone in his 62nd game of the year.

March 17, 2009

New Jersey's Martin Brodeur broke Patrick Roy's all-time record for wins by a goalie with the 552nd win of his career.

March 18, 1945

Maurice Richard became the first player in NHL history to score 50 goals in a single season — on the final night of the 1944–45 season. He led the Montreal Canadiens to a 4–2 win over Boston. He got a $500 bonus for the goal.

March 19, 2009

The first tournament for the Clarkson Cup began. The Canadian Women's Hockey Championship was won by the Montreal Stars two days later.

March 20, 1971

Two brothers faced each other in the nets for the only time in NHL history. Ken Dryden's Montreal Canadiens beat Dave Dryden's Buffalo Sabres 5–2.

Dryden vs. Dryden

Ken Dryden of the Montreal Canadiens was one of the best goalies in NHL history. In his eight NHL seasons he won the Stanley Cup six times. He also won the Vezina Trophy as the league's top goalie five times.

Dave Dryden made his NHL debut on February 3, 1962. He was a junior goalie in Toronto and was watching the game at Maple Leaf Gardens when New York Rangers goalie Gump Worsley

Ken Dryden (left) and his brother Dave (right)

got hurt. Teams didn't carry spare goalies back then, so the two teams agreed to let Dave take over.

In the 1970–71 season, Dave was a backup goalie with the Buffalo Sabres; the Canadiens had recently called up Ken from the minors. When the two teams met on March 20, Sabres coach Punch Imlach sent Dave out to start. He thought the Canadiens would start Ken too. When they didn't, Imlach pulled Dave after the first whistle. However, when Canadiens starting goalie Rogie Vachon got injured in the second period, Ken took over. The Sabres put Dave back in the net. When the game was over, fans cheered as the Dryden brothers shook hands at centre ice.

March 21, 1998

South Korea defeated Thailand 92–0 on the last day of the Asia-Oceania Under-18 Championships in Harbin, China. This is the highest-scoring game in any tournament ever organized by the International Ice Hockey Federation.

March 22, 1894

The first championship game in Stanley Cup history was played. Forward Billy Barlow scored twice to give the Montreal AAA a 3–1 win over Ottawa in a one-game Stanley Cup Final. Montreal had also won the Cup in 1893, but there was no playoff that year. They earned the Cup that year by finishing the regular season in first place in their league.

March 23, 1994

Wayne Gretzky scored his 802nd NHL career goal to move past Gordie Howe into first place. Commissioner Gary Bettman presented Gretzky with a book containing the score sheets from every game in which he had scored.

March 24, 1936

The Detroit Red Wings beat the Montreal Maroons 1–0 in the longest game in NHL history. The game lasted until 16:30 of the sixth overtime period.

March 25, 1990

Team Canada beat the United States 5–2 in the gold medal game to win the first official Women's World Championship.

March 26, 1917

The Seattle Metropolitans of the Pacific Coast Hockey Association became the first American team to win the Stanley Cup.

A Woman's World

Women have been playing hockey for a lot longer than most people think. One of the first women to play hockey in Canada was Isobel Stanley, Lord Stanley's daughter.

The 1931–32 Preston Rivulettes

By the late 1890s, women were playing hockey all across Canada. However, by the 1950s, people felt that hockey was too rough for women. Although there were women who played hockey in the 1960s and '70s, they had little support. Things finally started to improve during the 1980s.

In 1987 a Women's World Championship was held in Toronto. There were teams from Canada, the United States, Sweden, Switzerland, Holland and Japan. Team Canada won the gold medal, but the International Ice Hockey Federation did not recognize this as an official tournament. The first official Women's World Championship was held three years later in Ottawa. Team Canada wore bright pink uniforms. Although some of the women found the outfits embarrassing, they did help bring attention to the tournament.

March 27, 1985

Los Angeles Kings star Marcel Dionne scored a goal to become the third player in NHL history to reach the 1,500-point mark.

March 28, 1975

The Washington Capitals won their only road game of the 1974–75 season. The win snapped a 37-game road losing streak. The Capitals finished their first season in the NHL with a record of 1–39–0 on the road. Their record was 8–67–5 overall.

March 29, 1929

The Boston Bruins beat the New York Rangers 2–1 to win the Stanley Cup for the first time in franchise history. The 1929 series also marked the first time that two U.S. teams had met in the Stanley Cup Finals.

March 30, 1916

The Montreal Canadiens won their first Stanley Cup title. At the time, the Canadiens played in the National Hockey Association. The NHL hadn't been formed yet.

March 31, 1923

The Ottawa Senators beat the Edmonton Eskimos of the Western Canada Hockey League 1–0 to win the Stanley Cup. Ottawa's King Clancy is said to have played all six positions during the game. He even took over in the net for two minutes during the second period because Senators goalie Clint Benedict got sent to the penalty box for slashing.

April 1, 1978

Mike Bossy of the New York Islanders became the first rookie in NHL history to score 50 goals in a season. Bossy also scored his 51st with five seconds left in the game.

Who's the Boss?

Mike Bossy was a scoring sensation when he played in the Quebec Junior Hockey League. He had 309 goals in his junior career, but the league was rough. Bossy's talent meant he

Mike Bossy scores his 50th goal

was often picked on. He'd fight when he had to, but he never liked it. As a result, many scouts wondered if he was tough enough to make it in the NHL.

The New York Islanders picked Bossy 15th in the first round of the 1977 NHL draft. The following season he scored 53 goals. No rookie had ever scored 50 goals before. The next season, he led the NHL with 69 goals. He led the league again with 68 in 1980–81.

Bossy scored 50 goals or more for nine straight seasons. No one else in NHL history has ever put up a streak like that. His streak finally ended during the 1986–87 season when he suffered a back injury. He only got to play 10 seasons in the NHL, but he scored 573 goals in just 752 games. Bossy's goals per-game-rate of .762 is the highest in NHL history.

April 2, 1980

Edmonton's Wayne Gretzky became the youngest player in NHL history to score 50 goals in a season. Gretzky was just 19 years and two months old. Even though it was his first NHL season, Gretzky wasn't considered a rookie. That was because he had spent the 1978–79 season playing in the rival World Hockey Association.

April 3, 2008

Alex Ovechkin scored two goals to lead Washington past Tampa Bay 4–1. The goals were Ovechkin's 64th and 65th of the 2007–08 season. That broke Luc Robitaille's NHL record of 63 goals by a left winger.

April 4, 1987

New York Islanders star Denis Potvin became the first defenseman in NHL history to reach the 1,000-point plateau.

April 5, 2007

New Jersey's Martin Brodeur won his 48th game of the 2006–07 season. That set a NHL record for wins by a goalie in a season. Bernie Parent held the old record with 47 wins for the Philadelphia Flyers in 1973–74.

April 6, 1945

For the first time in Stanley Cup history, two rookie goaltenders faced each other in the Stanley Cup Finals. Frank McCool was in net for Toronto. Harry Lumley was the Detroit goalie. McCool got three shutouts in the series as the Leafs beat the Red Wings in seven games.

April 7, 2002

Calgary's Jarome Iginla scored his 50th goal of the 2001–02 season. It was the first time Iginla had reached the 50-goal plateau. He finished the season with a league-leading 52 goals and 96 points.

April 8, 1978

Bruins rookie Bob Miller scored his 20th goal of the season. Miller was the 11th Boston player to score 20 goals or more that year. Having eleven 20-goal scorers set an NHL record that has never been broken.

April 9, 1987

The Edmonton Oilers set an NHL playoff record for goals in a game. They beat Los Angeles 13–3.

April 10, 1934

Goalie Charlie Gardiner earned a shutout as Chicago beat Detroit 1–0 in double overtime to win the Stanley Cup. It was the first championship in Black Hawks history. Sadly, Gardiner died of a brain tumor just a few weeks later.

April 11, 1965

Norm Ullman scored two goals in five seconds to set a playoff record for fastest goals in a playoff game. Ullman scored at 17:35 and 17:40 of the second period to lead Detroit past Chicago 4–2.

April 12, 1941

For the first time since the NHL adopted the best-of-seven format in 1939, a team won the Stanley Cup in four straight games. Boston beat Detroit 3–1 to complete the series sweep.

April 13, 2006

Alex Ovechkin became the fourth rookie in NHL history to score 50 goals in a season. The first three were Mike Bossy, Joe Nieuwendyk and Teemu Selanne.

April 14, 1960

Goalie Jacques Plante shut out the Toronto Maple Leafs 4–0 as the Montreal Canadiens capped their fifth straight Stanley Cup title. No other team in NHL history has ever won the Stanley Cup five years in a row.

April 15, 1952

The Red Wings beat the Canadiens to complete a four-game sweep of the Stanley Cup Finals. Detroit had also swept Toronto in the semifinals. The Red Wings became the first NHL team to win eight straight games in one playoff year.

April 16, 1999

Wayne Gretzky announced his retirement after 20 seasons in the NHL. He played his final game two days later.

Five for Five

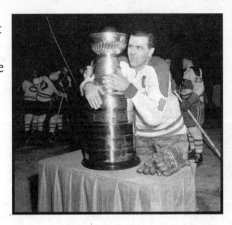

Some people say that hockey's greatest dynasty grew out of one of the game's darkest moments. On March 13, 1955, Maurice Richard punched a linesman during a fight. Three days later, NHL president Clarence Campbell suspended Richard, which meant that he would miss the last three games of the regular season and the playoffs. Fans rioted in the streets after Campbell showed up at a game at the Forum the next day.

A month after the riot, the Canadiens lost the seventh game of the 1955 Stanley Cup Finals to the Detroit Red Wings. But the Canadiens got their revenge in 1955–56. New coach Toe Blake helped Richard keep his fiery temper in check. The Canadiens set a new NHL record with 45 wins during the season. In the playoffs, they beat the Red Wings in the Finals to win the Stanley Cup.

The Canadiens went on to win the Cup five years in a row. In every season during their dynasty, Montreal led the NHL in scoring. They also had the fewest goals against. Twelve players from the 1955–56 Canadiens were still on the team in 1960 . . . including Maurice Richard.

April 17, 2006

Pittsburgh's Sidney Crosby became the youngest player in NHL history to score 100 points in a season. Crosby was 18 years and 253 days old when he reached the milestone.

April 18, 1942

The Toronto Maple Leafs completed the greatest comeback in Stanley Cup history. They won their fourth straight game of the Finals after losing the first three games to Detroit.

April 19, 1970

Phil Esposito scored a hat trick to lead Boston past Chicago 6–3 in the opening game of their semifinal playoff series. Brother Tony Esposito was in net for the Black Hawks.

April 20, 1934

Tommy Gorman resigned as coach and general manager of the Chicago Black Hawks. He had just led Chicago to a Stanley Cup title 10 days earlier. Two weeks later, Gorman was hired by the Montreal Maroons. He led them to the Stanley Cup Championship in 1935.

April 21, 1951

Toronto's Bill Barilko scored the Stanley Cup-winning goal in overtime to lead the Maple Leafs past the Canadiens. Every game in the five-game series was decided in overtime. Later that summer, Barilko died in a plane crash. His remains were not discovered until 1962. Spookily, the Leafs did not win the Cup again until that year.

Sid the Kid

Sidney Crosby started playing hockey when he was just two years old, and started playing hockey with the Dartmouth Timbits in Nova Scotia when he was just five.

Crosby became a local star when he was only 10 years old. When he was 14, he led his midget hockey team to the finals of the Canadian championship. Most of the other players on the team were 16 and 17 years old. By the time Crosby was 16, Wayne Gretzky had predicted that he might be the one to break his records one day. That year, Crosby was the top scorer in all of Canadian junior hockey. He also helped Team Canada win gold at the World Junior Championship. The next year, he did it all again.

No one was surprised when the Pittsburgh Penguins made Crosby the first pick in the 2005 NHL Entry Draft. There was a lot of pressure on him when he began his NHL career, but he certainly lived up to it: he became the youngest player to reach 100 points in a season, finishing with 39 goals and 63 assists for 102 points.

April 22, 1976

Darryl Sittler scored five goals to lead Toronto past Philadelphia 8–5. At the time, Sittler tied the NHL playoff record for most goals in one game held by Newsy Lalonde and Maurice Richard.

April 23, 1950

Detroit's Pete Babando became the first player to score an overtime goal in Game 7 of the Stanley Cup Finals. Babando's goal beat the Rangers 4–3. On April 16, 1954, Tony Leswick of the Red Wings became the only other player in history to win the Stanley Cup with an overtime goal in Game 7. Detroit beat the Canadiens that year.

April 24, 2006

Avalanche centre Joe Sakic scored in overtime to give Colorado a 5–4 win over Dallas. It was the seventh playoff overtime goal of Sakic's career. That broke the old record of six overtime goals Sakic had shared with Maurice Richard.

April 25, 1989

Mario Lemieux had five goals and three assists to lead Pittsburgh past Washington 10–7. Lemieux became the fifth player in NHL history to score five goals in one playoff game. He also tied the playoff record for most points in one game. New Jersey's Patrick Sundstrom had picked up eight points back on April 22, 1988.

April 26, 1920

The Winnipeg Falcons beat Sweden 12–1 to win the gold medal for Canada in the very first Olympic hockey tournament.

Dynasty Days

The NHL had just six teams between 1942 and 1967. Competition was fierce . . . but it wasn't very even. The Boston Bruins, New York Rangers and Chicago Black Hawks always struggled. Meanwhile, the Montreal Canadiens,

The Leafs win the 1967 Cup

Toronto Maple Leafs and Detroit Red Wings combined to win the Stanley Cup 24 times in 25 seasons.

Toronto was the first team in NHL history to win the Cup three years in a row, from 1947 to 1949. In 1951 they added their fourth win in five years.

After a win by the Black Hawks in 1961, the Maple Leafs moved back on top. Punch Imlach, the team's coach and general manager, had established stars like George Armstrong, Tim Horton and Frank Mahovlich on the team and was able to add further talent such as Dave Keon, Red Kelly and Terry Sawchuk. The team went on to win the Cup in 1962, 1963 and 1964. The Canadiens won it in 1965 and 1966, and some thought they'd make it three in a row. But the Leafs brought the Stanley Cup back to Toronto instead — the last time they ever won a Cup.

May 3, 1995

Pittsburgh's Jaromir Jagr became the first European-trained player to win the Art Ross Trophy as the NHL's scoring leader. In fact, he won the Art Ross Trophy four years in a row from 1997–98 through 2000–01.

May 4, 2009

Alex Ovechkin and Sidney Crosby both scored their first career playoff hat tricks in the same game. Ovechkin's Capitals beat Crosby's Penguins 4–3.

May 5, 1966

Henri Richard scored in overtime to give the Montreal Canadiens a Stanley Cup victory over Detroit in six games. Despite losing the series, Red Wings goalie Roger Crozier won the Conn Smythe Trophy as playoff MVP.

May 6, 1976

Two weeks after Darryl Sittler tied a playoff record with five goals against Philadelphia, Flyers star Reggie Leach scored five times to lead his team to a 6–3 win over Boston.

May 7, 1985

Edmonton's Jari Kurri scored three goals in a 7–3 playoff win over Chicago. It was the first of three hat tricks Kurri got against the Black Hawks in the series. That's a record for the most hat tricks in one playoff series.

Flying Finn

Jari Kurri feeds a pass to Wayne Gretzky

Growing up in Finland in the 1970s, Jari Kurri didn't know much about the NHL. After playing for Finland at the 1980 Winter Olympics, Kurri was drafted by the Edmonton Oilers. During his first season in the NHL, Kurri was put on Wayne Gretzky's line. Cashing in on Gretzky's great passes, Kurri scored 32 goals as a rookie in 1980–81.

Gretzky and Kurri helped make Edmonton the greatest offensive team in NHL history. In 1981–82, the Oilers became the first team to score 400 goals in a season. By the 1983–84 season, they had upped their record to 446. The Oilers also won the Stanley Cup for the first time that season. Kurri scored 52 goals. He had 71 the next season, and helped the Oilers repeat as Stanley Cup champions. In 1985–86 Kurri led the league with 68 goals.

Kurri helped the Oilers win the Stanley Cup again in 1987, 1988 and 1990. By the time he retired in 1998, Kurri had scored 601 goals and 1,398 points, making him the highest-scoring European player in NHL history at the time.

May 8, 1973
Chicago and Montreal combined to set an NHL record with 15 goals in one Stanley Cup game. The Black Hawks beat the Canadiens 8–7 in Game 5 of the Finals.

May 9, 1992
Pittsburgh won its first of a record 14-straight playoff games over two years. The Penguins finished the 1992 playoffs with 11 straight wins on their way to the Stanley Cup.

May 10, 1970
Bobby Orr scored 40 seconds into overtime in Game 4 to lead Boston to a sweep of St. Louis in the Stanley Cup Finals. It was the first time the Bruins had won the Stanley Cup since 1941.

May 11, 2003
Canada beat Sweden 3–2 in overtime to win the gold medal at the World Championship. Anson Carter scored the winning goal . . . although it took several minutes of video review to make sure the puck had really crossed the goal line. It was the first time the World title had ever been determined by video review.

May 12, 1973

The Toronto Maple Leafs signed Swedish players Borje Salming and Inge Hammarstrom as free agents. Salming was the first European player to become a star in the NHL.

May 13, 1980

Denis Potvin scored in overtime to give the New York Islanders a 4–3 win over Philadelphia in Game 1 of the Stanley Cup Finals. The last game of the series would end in overtime too. On May 24, 1980, Bob Nystrom's OT goal gave the Islanders their first Stanley Cup title.

May 14, 1927

The NHL officially accepted the Vezina Trophy as an award for the league's top goalie. The Montreal Canadiens donated the trophy to the league in honour of their star goalie Georges Vezina, who had died the year before.

May 15, 1990

Petr Klima scored at 15:13 of the third overtime period to end the longest game in the history of the Stanley Cup Finals. Edmonton beat Boston 3–2 in Game 1 of the series.

May 16, 1976

Philadelphia's Reggie Leach scored his 19th goal of the playoffs. The Canadiens still beat the Flyers 5–3 to sweep the Stanley Cup Finals, but Leach's new scoring record earned him the Conn Smythe Trophy as playoff MVP.

May 17, 1983
The New York Islanders beat the Oilers 4–2 to complete a four-game sweep of the 1983 Stanley Cup Finals. It was the Islanders' fourth straight Stanley Cup title, one short of the NHL record for consecutive championships set by the Montreal Canadiens from 1956 to 1960.

May 18, 1986
Brian Skrudland scored just nine seconds into overtime to give Montreal a 3–2 win over Calgary in Game 2 of the Stanley Cup Finals. It was the fastest overtime goal in NHL playoff history.

May 19, 1974
The Philadelphia Flyers became the first post-1967 expansion team to win the Stanley Cup, beating the Bruins 1–0 in Game 6 of the Finals.

May 20, 1993
The Montreal Canadiens won their seventh consecutive overtime game of the playoffs to set a new NHL record. The Canadiens would run their overtime winning streak to 10 straight games en route to capturing the Stanley Cup.

May 21, 2009
Evgeni Malkin scored his first career playoff hat trick. He led the Penguins past the Carolina Hurricanes 7–4 in game two of their Eastern Conference Final.

From Worst to First

The New York Islanders joined the NHL for the 1972–73 season. Their record that year was 12–60–6. Their 60 losses set a new NHL record. The only good thing about finishing last was getting to pick first in the NHL draft. The Islanders chose Denis Potvin. He quickly became one of the league's best defenseman.

By their third season, the Islanders had improved greatly. They made the playoffs, and even won two series. Soon, other draft picks like Clark Gillies, Bryan Trottier and Mike Bossy helped make the Islanders one of the best teams in the NHL. They topped 100 points in the standings four years in a row. Yet they kept going out early in the playoffs. Then, in just their eighth season in the NHL, the Islanders won their first Stanley Cup.

They went on to win the Cup four years in a row. They reached the Finals for a fifth straight time in 1984, but were beaten by the Edmonton Oilers. Before that loss, the Islanders had won 19 playoff series in a row — something that has never been done.

May 22, 1970
Buffalo and Vancouver were officially granted NHL expansion teams for the 1970–71 season.

May 23, 1991
Pittsburgh's Larry Murphy tied two records in the Stanley Cup Finals. He got three assists in the first period, and four in the game.

May 24, 1986
The Montreal Canadiens won the Stanley Cup for the 23rd time in franchise history. At the time, this set a professional record for the most championship seasons. Montreal had been tied with baseball's New York Yankees, who had won the World Series 22 times.

May 25, 1989
The Calgary Flames captured their first Stanley Cup title. Calgary beat the Montreal Canadiens 4–2 in Game 6 to wrap up the series.

May 26, 2000
The New Jersey Devils defeated the Philadelphia Flyers 2–1 in Game 7 of the Eastern Conference Final, becoming the first team to rally from a three-games-to-one series deficit to reach the Stanley Cup Finals.

The Battle of Alberta

Lanny McDonald cradles the Cup

The cities of Calgary and Edmonton have been rivals for a long time. The rivalry dates all the way back to the 1880s when the Canadian Pacific Railway decided to run its tracks through Calgary instead of Edmonton. The two cities were still fighting 100 years later . . . although the biggest battles in Alberta in the 1980s were always on the ice.

Between 1983 and 1990, either the Calgary Flames or the Edmonton Oilers reached the Stanley Cup Finals every year. They often met up in the playoffs. It was a pretty good bet that whichever team survived their battle would wind up winning the Stanley Cup. Usually, it was the Oilers. But in 1986 Calgary upset Edmonton in the second round in a tough, seven-game series. The Flames won the final game when Oilers defenseman Steve Smith scored a goal on his own net.

Edmonton knocked Calgary out of the playoffs again in 1988, but the Flames finally won the Cup in 1989. Stars like Joe Mullen, Joe Nieuwendyk, Doug Gilmour and Al MacInnis led the team . . . though it was veteran Lanny McDonald who scored the Cup-winning goal.

May 27, 1994

After Mark Messier guaranteed fans the Rangers would win in Game 6 — which they did — the Rangers went on to win Game 7 against the New Jersey Devils 2–1 in of the Eastern Conference Final in double overtime. A record three games in the series were decided in double overtime.

May 28, 2002

Martin Gelinas scored in overtime to take the Carolina Hurricanes into the Stanley Cup Finals for the first time. The goal gave Carolina a 2–1 win over Toronto.

May 29, 1993

Wayne Gretzky scored a hat trick to lead Los Angeles to a 5–4 win over Toronto in Game 7 of the Western Conference Final. It was Gretzky's eighth career playoff hat trick, breaking the record of seven he'd shared with Maurice Richard and Jari Kurri.

May 30, 1985

Jari Kurri scored his 19th goal of the playoffs, tying Reggie Leach's postseason record, as the Edmonton Oilers beat Philadelphia 8–3 to wrap up their second straight Stanley Cup title.

May 31, 2004

Tampa Bay's Brad Richards set a new NHL record with his seventh game-winning goal in one playoff year. Richards got the only goal in a 1–0 win over Calgary in Game 4 of the Stanley Cup Finals.

Right On the Mark

Mark Messier became a star with the Edmonton Oilers in the 1980s. He became a legend with the New York Rangers in 1994.

Messier won the Stanley Cup four times with the Oilers in the 1980s. After Wayne Gretzky was traded in 1988, Messier led the team to another championship in 1990. The Rangers hoped he could do the same thing for them when they signed him in 1991.

The Rangers finished the 1993–94 season in first place. They knocked off the Islanders and the Capitals in the first two rounds of the playoffs, but ran into trouble against the Devils in the Eastern Conference Final. New Jersey was up 3–2 in the series heading into Game 6. Messier promised the media that the Rangers would win . . . and made good on his promise. He scored three goals in the third period for a 4–2 win. They wrapped up the series with Stephane Matteau's double overtime winner in the seventh game.

The Rangers faced the Canucks in the Stanley Cup Finals. They jumped out to a 3–1 lead in the series, but almost let it slip away. When they won 3–2 in Game 7, it was Mark Messier who scored the winning goal.

June 1, 1992

The first NHL game to take place in June was played. Pittsburgh beat Chicago 6–5, giving the Penguins a sweep of the Stanley Cup Finals. It was the second year in a row that Pittsburgh had won the Stanley Cup.

June 2, 1948

The NHL announced that the Art Ross Trophy would be given to the league's leading scorer. Before that, there had been no such trophy.

June 3, 1993

Eric Desjardins of the Canadiens became the first defenseman in NHL history to record a hat trick in the Stanley Cup Finals.

June 4, 1996

The 1996 Stanley Cup Finals opened with the Colorado Avalanche defeating the Florida Panthers 3–1 in Denver. This was the first time in NHL history that both teams in the Finals had never played for the Stanley Cup.

June 5, 2006

Chris Pronger of the Edmonton Oilers became the first player in the history of the Stanley Cup Finals to score a goal on a penalty shot. Pronger beat Carolina's Cam Ward . . . but the Hurricanes still won the game 5–4.

June 6, 2007

The Anaheim Ducks captured their first Stanley Cup title, becoming the first team from California to win it. They beat the Ottawa Senators 6–2 in Game 5 of the Finals.

June 7, 1972

Gordie Howe and Jean Béliveau were among five players elected to the Hockey Hall of Fame. Both Howe and Béliveau got into the Hall without the usual three-year waiting period after a player retires.

Hall of Fame

I t's something reserved for the greats of the game: induction into the Hockey Hall of Fame.

There's a special Selection Committee that decides which players are chosen for induction into the Hall. The rules state that a player must be retired for three years before he is eligible for induction. However, there have been some exceptions over the years.

Bobby Orr gives his induction speech

Dit Clapper was the first to be inducted earlier than the three-year waiting period, in 1947. The next player to be so honoured was Maurice Richard in 1961. "The Rocket" was the NHL's all-time leader with 544 goals when he announced his retirement in September of 1960. The Hall of Fame building was set to open the following summer and inducting Richard was thought to be a fitting dedication.

Over the years, eight more players received this early honour "by reason of outstanding pre-eminence and skill": Ted Lindsay (1966), Red Kelly (1969), Terry Sawchuk (1971), Jean Béliveau (1972), Gordie Howe (1972), Bobby Orr (1979), Mario Lemieux (1997) and Wayne Gretzky (1999). After Gretzky was inducted, the Hall of Fame announced that it would no longer waive the three-year waiting period for anyone.

June 8, 1996

A Stanley Cup game was played in Florida for the first time. The visiting Colorado Avalanche rallied to defeat the Florida Panthers 3–2 at the Miami Arena.

June 9, 1993

The Montreal Canadiens beat the Los Angeles Kings to win the Stanley Cup for the 24th time in franchise history. Patrick Roy won the Conn Smythe Trophy as playoff MVP for the second time in his career.

June 10, 1996

The Avalanche became the first team in NHL history to win the Stanley Cup in their first year in a new city. They had just moved to Denver after 16 seasons as the Quebec Nordiques.

June 11, 1969

The Chicago Black Hawks claimed Tony Esposito from the Montreal Canadiens for $25,000. He would set a modern hockey record with 15 shutouts for Chicago in 1969–70, and go on to become one of the best goalies in NHL history.

June 12, 2009

At age 21, Pittsburgh's Sidney Crosby became the youngest captain to hoist the Stanley Cup when the Penguins defeated the Detroit Red Wings. Pittsburgh's Evgeni Malkin also became the first Russian to win the Conn Smythe Trophy as playoff MVP.

June 13, 1974

Don Cherry was named coach of the Boston Bruins. As a player, Cherry spent 16 years in the minor leagues and played only one game in the NHL. As a coach, he led Boston to four division titles in his five seasons. He won the Jack Adams Award as coach of the year in 1975–76, but never won the Stanley Cup.

June 14, 1994

The New York Rangers won the Stanley Cup for the first time in 54 years, beating Vancouver 3–2 in Game 7.

Jinx!

When the New York Rangers won the Stanley Cup in 1940, it was the third time the team had won the championship in just 14 seasons in the NHL. But

The New York Rangers and the 1940 Stanley Cup

their next Stanley Cup victory wouldn't come for another 54 years. Some fans believed the Rangers were cursed.

Stories said that Red Dutton had cursed the Rangers. For many years, Dutton had run the New York Americans. They were the first NHL team in New York, but they never had the same success as the Rangers. Dutton supposedly cursed the Rangers when the Americans were forced to drop out of the NHL in 1942.

There is an even more famous story about how the Rangers got cursed. During the 1940–41 season, the bank loan to build the old Madison Square Garden was finally paid off. The owners decided to burn their mortgage papers inside the bowl of the Stanley Cup. According to legend, this act angered the hockey gods . . . and that's why it took the Rangers so long to win the Cup again.

June 15, 1985

The 1985 NHL Entry Draft was held in Toronto. The Maple Leafs
had the first pick, and selected Wendel Clark, who would one
day become the team's captain.

June 16, 1998

Detroit won the Stanley Cup for the second year in a row. For Red
Wings coach Scotty Bowman, it was the eighth Stanley Cup victory
of his career. That tied him with Toe Blake for the most wins by a
coach. Bowman broke the record with his ninth Cup win in 2002.

June 17, 1989

Mats Sundin became the first European player to be selected
number one in the NHL Entry Draft. The young Swedish star was
selected first overall by the Quebec Nordiques.

June 18, 1989

Though he had never played in the NHL, Soviet goalie Vladislav
Tretiak became the first European player to be elected to the
Hockey Hall of Fame.

From Russia With Love

Vladislav Tretiak was one of hockey's greatest goaltenders.

Tretiak started playing hockey when he was 11. By the time he was 15, he was practicing with Moscow's Central

Tretiak makes a save against Team Canada

Red Army, the best team in the Soviet Union. He joined them in 1968 when he was just 17 and helped them win 13 league championships over the next 16 years.

Tretiak came to the attention of hockey fans in North America with his brilliant play during the 1972 Summit Series between Team Canada and the Soviets. He was named MVP when the Soviets won the Canada Cup in 1981, and won the Golden Stick award as the outstanding player in Europe three years in a row, from 1981 to 1983.

When he retired after the 1983–84 season, Tretiak had played for 10 World Champion teams with the Soviet national team and won three Olympic gold medals. In 98 World Championship games, he boasted a goals-against average of 1.92 — he had a 1.74 in 19 Olympic Games. In 2006 Tretiak became the head of the Russian Ice Hockey Federation.

June 19, 1973
Two years after he left the NHL, Gordie Howe came out of retirement and signed with the Houston Aeros of the World Hockey Association. His sons Mark and Marty also signed with the Aeros. The Howes were the first father-and-son combination to play together on the same team in any professional sport.

June 20, 1995
The New Jersey Devils tied a playoff record with their seventh straight win on the road beating Detroit 4–2 in Game 2 of the Stanley Cup Finals.

June 21, 1999
The NHL announced new rules for overtime in the regular season. Teams would play with four skaters and a goalie. Also, the losing team would get a point if the game was won in overtime. (Shootouts weren't introduced until the 2005–06 season.)

June 22, 1979
The NHL grew from 17 teams to 21 when the league took in four teams from the World Hockey Association. The four teams were the Edmonton Oilers, the Quebec Nordiques, the Winnipeg Jets and the Hartford Whalers.

June 23, 2006
The Vancouver Canucks acquired Roberto Luongo in a trade with the Florida Panthers. Luongo went on to become one of the top goalies in the NHL.

A Whole New World

Bobby Hull

When the World Hockey Association started in 1972, it marked the first time in many years that the NHL had a rival. No one had really tried to challenge the NHL since the collapse of the Western Hockey League back in 1926.

The WHA changed a lot about hockey. The NHL added several expansion teams in the 1970s to try and beat the WHA into new hockey markets. But the WHA offered its players bigger contracts, so the NHL was forced to pay more money to its own players. At the start of the 1970s, the average salary in the NHL was only $18,000. By the start of the 1980s, it had grown to more than $100,000.

Bobby Hull was the biggest star to join the WHA. He also got a big contract. Soon, more NHL players were joining the new league. Many players who had never done very well in the NHL became big stars in the WHA. The new league was also faster to welcome players from Europe than the NHL and even let Wayne Gretzky play when he was only 17 years old. The WHA lasted for seven seasons. Four of its teams — and many of its players — joined the NHL in 1979.

July 2, 2001

The Minnesota Wild signed free agent defenseman Jason Marshall and free agent goaltender Dwayne Roloson. The Wild dealt Roloson to the Edmonton Oilers at the NHL trade deadline in 2006.

July 3, 1970

Teemu Selanne was born in Helsinki, Finland. Selanne set an NHL record for rookies when he scored 76 goals for the Winnipeg Jets in 1992–93.

July 4, 2007

The Calgary Flames signed Jarome Iginla to a five-year contract extension worth $35 million. The new deal started with the 2008–09 season and runs through 2012–13.

July 5, 2000

Dave King signed as the first head coach in Columbus Blue Jackets history.

July 6, 2004

Goalie Dominik Hasek signed as a free agent with the Ottawa Senators. Hasek had led Detroit to the Stanley Cup in 2002. Previously, with the Buffalo Sabres, Hasek had been the first goalie in NHL history to win the Hart Trophy as league MVP twice.

July 7, 1998

Canadian women's team star Hayley Wickenheiser joined the Philadelphia Flyers for their eight-day rookie camp.

The Finnish Flash

Nobody in NHL history has burst onto the scene like Teemu Selanne. In his first season of 1992–93, Selanne set a rookie record for goals that may never be matched.

The Winnipeg Jets selected Selanne 10th overall at the 1988 NHL Draft. It took him four years to leave his home in Finland, but it was well worth the wait. In his first game in 1992, Selanne picked up his first assist. His first goal came two nights later . . . and Selanne just kept on scoring. Mike Bossy had held the NHL rookie record for goals with 53 — Selanne scored his 54th with more than a month left in the season. At the end of the season, Selanne had 76 goals. Only three players in NHL history had ever scored more. Selanne finished with 132 points, setting another rookie record.

Though he never matched the huge numbers of his first season, Selanne continued to be a dangerous offensive player. When he scored 48 goals for the Anaheim Ducks in 2006–07, it was the seventh time in his career that he'd scored 40 or more. At the age of 36, Selanne was the oldest player in NHL history to score more than 45 goals in a single season.

July 8, 1995

The 1995 NHL Entry Draft was held in Edmonton. Ottawa had the first pick and selected Bryan Berard. Later, they traded him to the Islanders for a second pick, Wade Redden. Shane Doan was the seventh choice in that year's draft. Jarome Iginla was picked 11th.

July 9, 1997

The expansion team Nashville Predators named David Poile as the team's first general manager.

July 10, 2007

The Penguins signed Sidney Crosby to a five-year contract extension worth $43.5 million. Crosby's new deal began in 2008–09 and runs through 2012–13. The contract paid Crosby an average of $8.7 million per season . . . matching his number 87.

July 11, 1963

Al MacInnis was born in Port Hood, Nova Scotia. He played 23 years in the NHL from 1981–82 until 2003–04, and had the hardest slap shot in hockey. MacInnis was elected to the Hockey Hall of Fame in 2007.

July 12, 1972

Team Canada named its 35-man roster for the upcoming Summit Series with the Soviet Union. The series would begin on September 2 and become the most famous series in hockey history.

July 13, 2007

Brent Sutter was hired as coach of the New Jersey Devils. Sutter had coached Team Canada to gold medals at the World Junior Championship in 2005 and 2006. He was one of six Sutter brothers to play in the NHL, and the fourth to become an NHL coach.

July 14, 1976

The NHL officially approved the sale of the California Seals to Cleveland, Ohio. The team became the Cleveland Barons. It was the first time an NHL team had moved to a new city since the original Ottawa Senators became the St. Louis Eagles in 1934.

Master Blaster

Though he was their first-round pick in the 1981 NHL Draft, the Calgary Flames didn't rush Al MacInnis. He didn't spend his first full season with the Flames until 1984–85. He soon became one of the league's best defensemen.

When Calgary won the Stanley Cup in 1989, MacInnis led all playoff performers in scoring. He was the first defenseman to do that in 11 years, and he became just the fourth defenseman in history to win the Conn Smythe Trophy as playoff MVP. During the 1990–91 season, MacInnis joined Bobby Orr, Denis Potvin and Paul Coffey as the only defensemen in NHL history to top 100 points in a season.

Yet what people remember most about MacInnis was his slap shot. Using an old-fashioned wooden stick, MacInnis could blast the puck 160 kilometres per hour. He won the Hardest Shot competition at the NHL All-Star Game seven times.

MacInnis had been working on his shot ever since he was nine years old: "I never thought it would end up the way it did and I'd be known for my slap shot."

July 15, 1997

Colorado Avalanche coach Marc Crawford was named coach of Team Canada for the 1998 Winter Olympics. The Games, held in Nagano, Japan, would mark the first time the NHL shut down its season so that players could compete at the Olympics.

July 16, 1988

Oilers superstar Wayne Gretzky married actress Janet Jones at a lavish wedding ceremony in Edmonton. Hundreds of guests were invited, and thousands of fans lined the streets outside the church.

July 17, 1994

The St. Louis Blues hired Mike Keenan as their new coach and general manager. Keenan had quit as Rangers coach two days before . . . just one month after leading the team to the Stanley Cup.

July 18, 2003

Detroit's Sergei Fedorov won the first Kharlamov Trophy, which goes to the best Russian player in the NHL. (See August 27, 1981)

The NHL Goes to the Olympics

Although future NHL players had appeared at every Olympic hockey tournament since the first one in 1920, active NHL players weren't allowed to compete until 1988, but only a few players participated. Teams had to agree to let their players go to the Olympics while the NHL season was still on. Canada added five active NHL players to its roster.

Dominik Hasek

The 1998 Winter Olympics in Nagano, Japan, marked the first time that every NHL player was eligible to play at the Olympics. The NHL agreed to shut down its season for two weeks in February so that players could participate. A total of 122 NHL players were able to represent their various countries in Nagano.

Fans in North America had high hopes for Team Canada and the United States. However, the U.S. didn't make it past the quarterfinals. Canada reached the semifinals, but lost 2–1 to the Czech Republic in a shootout.

The Czechs faced Russia in the final game. The Canucks' Pavel Bure had scored nine goals for Russia in just five games, but he wasn't able to get one past Dominik Hasek. The Czechs beat Russia 1–0, winning the gold medal.

July 19, 1892

Dick Irvin was born in Hamilton, Ontario. Irvin was a star player in the 1910s and '20s who became an outstanding coach with the Toronto Maple Leafs and Montreal Canadiens in the 1930s, '40s and '50s. His son, who is also named Dick Irvin, is a Hockey Hall of Fame broadcaster.

July 20, 1990

The Pittsburgh Penguins signed Bryan Trottier as a free agent. The former New York Islanders star was one of the top scorers in hockey history. He'd won the Stanley Cup four times with the Islanders, and would help the Penguins win it twice.

July 21, 1996

The New York Rangers announced they had signed Wayne Gretzky as a free agent. The Rangers were Gretzky's fourth — and final — NHL team.

July 22, 2005

The NHL held a lottery with all 30 teams to determine the order of selection for the 2005 NHL Entry Draft. Pittsburgh won the top spot and picked Sidney Crosby when the Draft was held eight days later. (See July 30, 2005)

The Penguins Win the Lottery

The order of selection at the NHL Entry Draft is based on the NHL standings. To make sure that nobody tries to finish last just to get the first draft pick, a lottery is used. Still, the worse that a team does, the more chances it has of picking first. And to keep things fair, no team can move up more than four positions. That means one of the league's five worst teams will always get the first pick.

But what happens if there aren't any NHL standings? That happened in 2005. The 2004–05 season had been cancelled by a lockout. Some believed the NHL should just use the same order from the 2004 Draft. Others thought there should be a new lottery based on the standings from the 2003–04 season. But that would mean only five teams had a chance to get the top pick . . . and everyone knew that the top pick in 2005 was going to be Sidney Crosby. Every team wanted a chance to draft him.

So the NHL came up with a lottery system that was fair to everyone. The Penguins — which had been one of the league's worst teams — won and picked Crosby.

July 23, 1957

The Detroit Red Wings traded two future Hall of Famers to Chicago in one deal. The Black Hawks got Ted Lindsay and Glenn Hall. In return, Detroit got Johnny Wilson, Hank Bassen, Forbes Kennedy and Bill Preston . . . some good players, but no real stars.

July 24, 1924

Dudley "Red" Garrett was born in Toronto. He played briefly with the New York Rangers in 1942–43 before joining the Navy during World War II. He was killed in action on November 24, 1944. The award for rookie of the year in the American Hockey League is named in his honour.

July 25, 2007

After picking him first in the 2007 NHL Entry Draft, the Chicago Blackhawks signed Patrick Kane to his first contract.

July 26, 1972

Gerry Cheevers agreed to sign with the Cleveland Crusaders of the World Hockey Association. Cheevers had helped Boston win the Stanley Cup in 1970 and 1972. His goalie mask with stitches on it gave him one of the most famous "faces" in hockey.

July 27, 1995

In a blockbuster trade, St. Louis dealt All-Star left winger Brendan Shanahan to the Hartford Whalers for promising young defenseman Chris Pronger.

July 28, 1998

The Vancouver Canucks announced they had signed Mark Messier as a free agent. At the time, it was the richest deal in hockey history. Messier signed a three-year contract worth nearly $21 million.

July 29, 1925

Ted Lindsay was born in Renfrew, Ontario. Lindsay starred in the NHL for 17 seasons, mostly with the Detroit Red Wings and usually on a line with Gordie Howe.

July 30, 2005

The Pittsburgh Penguins selected Sidney Crosby as the first pick at the 2005 NHL Entry Draft held in Ottawa.

July 31, 1986

Evegni Malkin was born in Magnitogorsk, in the Soviet Union. Pittsburgh picked him second overall in the 2004 NHL Entry Draft, right behind Alex Ovechkin. Malkin joined the Penguins in 2006–07.

August 1, 2005

Randy Carlyle was hired as coach of the Anaheim Ducks. Carlyle played 17 seasons in the NHL without ever winning the Stanley Cup, but won it in just his second season as a coach, in 2006–07.

August 2, 2007

The Edmonton Oilers signed free agent forward Dustin Penner, who had just helped the Anaheim Ducks win the Stanley Cup. He was a restricted free agent, so the Oilers had to give Anaheim three draft picks.

August 3, 1951

Marcel Dionne was born in Drummondville, Quebec. He starred in the NHL for 18 seasons, mostly with the Los Angeles Kings. Dionne was the third player in NHL history to top 700 goals and the third to reach 1,000 assists.

August 4, 2005

After starring with the New Jersey Devils for 13 seasons, Scott Niedermayer signed with the Anaheim Ducks. Niedermayer won the Conn Smythe Trophy as playoff MVP as he helped lead Anaheim to the Stanley Cup in 2007.

August 5, 1937

Herb Brooks was born in St. Paul, Minnesota. In 1960 he was the last player cut from the U.S. Olympic hockey team that went on to win a surprising gold medal. In 1980 he coached the U.S. Olympic team to an even more surprising gold medal victory.

West Coast Winners

When Anaheim won the Stanley Cup in 2007, they became the first team from California to win hockey's most prized trophy. They were the first West Coast winners in NHL history . . . but

not the first in hockey history.

NHL teams have been the only ones to compete for the Stanley Cup since 1927. However, in the early days of hockey, other leagues could play for the Stanley Cup, too. The Vancouver Millionaires were members of the Pacific Coast Hockey Association (PCHA) when they won the Stanley Cup in 1915. Their victory marked the first time that the Stanley Cup went to a team further west than Winnipeg, which had won the Cup in the 1890s and 1900s. Two years later, in 1917, the Seattle Metropolitans won the Stanley Cup. The Mets, as they were known, also played in the PCHA. They were the first team from an American city to win the Stanley Cup.

In 1925 the Victoria Cougars of the Western Canada Hockey League won the Stanley Cup. The Cougars were the last non-NHL team ever to win the Stanley Cup.

August 6, 2004

The Phoenix Coyotes announced the signing of free agent Brett Hull. Phoenix was the last stop in a playing career that saw Hull score 741 goals . . . the third-highest total in NHL history.

August 7, 1987

Sidney Crosby was born in Cole Harbour, Nova Scotia. Crosby wears the number 87 because he was born in the eighth month, on the seventh day, in the year 1987.

August 8, 1992

The Tampa Bay Lightning signed goalie Manon Rheaume to a contract, making her the first woman to sign in the NHL. She would make her debut in an exhibition game on September 23, 1992, but never played in the regular season.

August 9, 1988

In a move that stunned hockey fans in Canada, the Edmonton Oilers traded Wayne Gretzky to the Los Angeles Kings. The Gretzky trade helped to make hockey a more popular game in the United States.

August 10, 1989

Corey Millen finally signed with the New York Rangers . . . seven years after the team drafted him in 1982.

August 11, 1920

Chuck Rayner was born in Sutherland, Saskatchewan. Rayner won the Hart Trophy as NHL MVP for the 1949–50 season, becoming the second goalie in history to win the award.

August 12, 1981

Serge Savard announced his retirement after 15 seasons with the Montreal Canadiens. Savard had helped the team win the Stanley Cup eight times. In 1969 he became the first defenseman to win the Conn Smythe Trophy as playoff MVP. In October 1981 Savard decided to return to the NHL and played two seasons with the Winnipeg Jets. He retired again in 1983.

Ladies First

Like many female hockey players, Manon Rheaume had to play with boys while growing up. When she was 11, she was the first girl at the Quebec International Peewee Tournament.

On November 26, 1991, Rheaume became the first woman to play major junior hockey in Canada. She played with the Trois-Rivières Draveurs in the Quebec Major Junior Hockey League. However, a shot to her head cut her through her mask, and she left the ice bleeding. Though she never played for the team again, her one appearance earned lots of attention.

Later in the 1991–92 season, Rheaume helped Team Canada win a gold medal at the Women's World Championship. The Tampa Bay Lightning then signed Rheaume to a contract, and invited her to training camp. On September 23, 1992, she played the first period of an exhibition game against the St. Louis Blues. Rheaume became the first woman to play in any of the four major professional sports leagues in North America.

Rheaume spent the next few seasons playing hockey for men's teams in the minor leagues and with the Canadian women's team. She retired in 2000.

August 13, 1949
Bobby Clarke was born in Flin Flon, Manitoba. He was diagnosed with Type 1 diabetes at age 15, but went on to star in the NHL with the Philadelphia Flyers for 15 seasons. He captained the team to the Stanley Cup twice and won the Hart Trophy as league MVP three times.

August 14, 1972
Team Canada opened its training camp for the upcoming Summit Series with the Soviet Union.

August 15, 1958
Craig MacTavish was born in London, Ontario. MacTavish played 17 years in the NHL. When he retired after the 1996–97 season, he was the last player in the league to play without wearing a helmet.

August 16, 1987
Carey Price was born in Anahim Lake, British Columbia. During his rookie season with the Montreal Canadiens in 2007–08, Price became the first goalie in 20 years to win 20 games at the age of 20 or younger.

August 17, 1992
Bryan Trottier retired after 18 seasons as an NHL player to become the Executive Assistant to the President of the New York Islanders. Trottier is the all-time leading scorer in Islanders history.

History of the Helmet

George Owen may have been the first NHL player to wear a helmet. Owen had played football and hockey at Harvard University and is said to have worn a leather football helmet during his rookie season with the Bruins.

Craig MacTavish

After Leafs forward Ace Bailey fractured his skull during a game in Boston, other Bruins began wearing helmets during the 1933–34 season. However, helmets remained unpopular. Not until Bill Masterton died of a head injury in 1968 did people begin to change their minds. Still, most players didn't wear them well into the 1970s.

During the 1970s, rules were passed to make helmets mandatory in junior leagues and the college ranks. Many of these players kept their helmets on when they reached the NHL. So did the players who joined the NHL from Europe, where they had always worn them. Finally, in 1979, the NHL passed a rule making helmets mandatory. However, anyone who had signed a contract before June 1, 1979 didn't have to wear one. By the 1995–96 season, Craig MacTavish was the last player left in the NHL who wasn't wearing a helmet.

August 18, 1994

Doug Gilmour was named captain of the Toronto Maple Leafs. He was just the 15th player in team history to receive the honour. During the 1992–93 season, Gilmour set Leafs records for most assists (95) and most points (127) in a season. He also won the Selke Trophy as the league's best defensive forward.

August 19, 1958

Darryl Sutter was born in Viking, Alberta. He was the fourth of six Sutter brothers to play in the NHL when he became a regular with the Chicago Black Hawks in 1980–81. Sutter scored 40 goals as a rookie that season. He became general manager of the Calgary Flames in 2003.

August 20, 1976

Chris Drury was born in Trumbull, Connecticut. In 1999, playing with the Colorado Avalanche, he won the Calder Trophy as the NHL's rookie of the year.

August 21, 1969

The Hockey Hall of Fame inducted five new members: Red Kelly, Sid Abel, Roy Worters, Bryan Hextall and builder Bruce Norris.

August 22, 1974

Tommy Dunderdale was elected to the Hockey Hall of Fame. Although he grew up in Ottawa and Winnipeg, Dunderdale is the only Honoured Member of the Hall of Fame to have been born in Australia. He was a professional hockey star in the 1910s and '20s.

August 23, 2005

Ottawa got Dany Heatley in a trade with the Atlanta Thrashers. The Senators sent Marian Hossa and Greg de Vries to Atlanta in the deal.

August 24, 1980

Brothers Peter and Anton Stastny defected from Czechoslovakia to join the NHL's Quebec Nordiques. Peter and Anton, and a third brother named Marian, all became stars in the NHL. Peter was one of the league's best players during the 1980s.

A Flight to Freedom

The 1972 Summit Series between Canada and the Soviet Union opened the NHL's eyes to the talent available in Europe. Over the next few years, many NHL teams began signing European players, mostly from Sweden and Finland. It was no problem for these players to leave their homelands.

The three Stastny brothers

However, hockey players from the Soviet Union and Czechoslovakia were unable to leave their countries freely. The only way out was to defect, which meant sneaking away and never going back.

Brothers Peter and Anton Stastny were star players in Czechoslovakia. The Quebec Nordiques had drafted Anton, and both brothers wanted the chance to play hockey in the NHL. During a summer hockey tournament in Austria in 1980, Peter contacted the Nordiques and told team president Marcel Aubut that he and his brother would sign with Quebec if the Nordiques could sneak them out of Europe. Aubut flew to Austria right away.

After the last game of the tournament, Aubut hid Peter, his wife and Anton in his car and drove them to Vienna. He got the proper papers from the Canadian embassy there, and flew them all to Canada.

August 25, 1939
Babe Siebert drowned while swimming in Lake Huron on a family vacation. The long-time NHL star had been named coach of the Montreal Canadiens earlier that summer.

August 26, 1961
The original Hockey Hall of Fame building opened on the Canadian National Exhibition grounds in Toronto.

August 27, 1981
Soviet hockey star Valeri Kharlamov died in a car accident near Moscow. Kharlamov was one of the greatest players in Russian history and was a star in the 1972 Summit Series. Ilya Kovalchuk wears number 17 in the NHL because that was the number Kharlamov wore.

August 28, 1989
Lanny McDonald retired after 16 seasons in the NHL. During his final season, McDonald scored his 500th career goal, recorded his 1,000th career point and won the Stanley Cup for the first time.

August 29, 1994
After four years of medical problems, including a battle with cancer, Penguins superstar Mario Lemieux announced he would sit out the entire 1994–95 season. But he returned to the ice in 1995–96 and won the Art Ross Trophy as the league's leading scorer.

Hallowed Halls

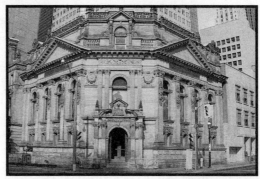

The Hockey Hall of Fame in downtown Toronto

Baseball was the first major sport to come up with the idea for a Hall of Fame. Players began being inducted in 1936, and in 1939 the National Baseball Hall of Fame and Museum officially opened in Cooperstown, New York.

James T. Sutherland, of Kingston, Ontario, was the first to suggest a Hockey Hall of Fame. With the support of the NHL and the Canadian Amateur Hockey Association, the Hockey Hall of Fame began inducting its first members in 1945.

Sutherland had hoped that the Hall would be built in Kingston. But after Sutherland died in 1955, attention shifted to Toronto. Maple Leafs owner Conn Smythe was put in charge of a plan to construct a Hall of Fame building on the grounds of the Canadian National Exhibition. Construction finally got started in 1960. Hockey legend Cyclone Taylor was given the honour of breaking the ground to get the work underway. The building opened one year later, on August 26, 1961.

On June 18, 1993, the Hall of Fame opened a new home in the heart of downtown Toronto.

August 30, 1994

The Montreal Canadiens named Kirk Muller as their new team captain. He became the 20th player in team history to wear the 'C' for the Canadiens.

August 31, 1975

John Grahame was born in Denver, Colorado. Grahame is the only player in hockey history to have had his name on the Stanley Cup along with his mother. Grahame was a backup goalie for Tampa Bay when they won the Stanley Cup in 2004. His mother, Charlotte Grahame, worked in the front office for Colorado when they won the Cup in 2001.

September 1, 1994

Paul Kariya signed his first NHL contract with the Anaheim Ducks. Kariya had been Anaheim's first draft choice (fourth overall) when they entered the NHL in 1993.

September 2, 1972

The first game of the eight-game Summit Series between Team Canada and the Soviet Union was played at the Montreal Forum. The Soviets won 7–3.

September 3, 1966

Bobby Orr signed his first NHL contract with the Boston Bruins when he was just 18 years old. Orr got a two-year deal for $75,000. At the time, it was the richest rookie contract in NHL history.

September 4, 1946

Clarence Campbell was named President of the NHL (a job now called commissioner). He would hold the job until 1977, making him the longest-serving head of the NHL.

September 5, 1959

Three new members were elected to the Hockey Hall of Fame: Jack Adams, Cy Denneny and Cecil "Tiny" Thompson.

Bobby's St-Orr-y

Many people believe Bobby Orr was the best player in hockey history.

Orr first began attracting attention at a bantam tournament in 1960 when he was 12 years old. He signed with the Boston Bruins when he was just 14 and spent the next four seasons playing with Boston's junior team, the Oshawa Generals. He shattered scoring records for junior defensemen, and was a First-Team All-Star three times.

During the summer of 1966, it was time to negotiate Orr's first NHL contract. The standard rookie salary was $8,000. The Bruins offered that, plus a $5,000 bonus. But Orr was one of the first hockey players to use an agent. He wound up signing a two-year deal worth $75,000.

Orr played only nine full seasons, but he won the Norris Trophy as best defenseman eight times. He was the first defenseman in NHL history to score 100 points in a season and the first player in history to top 100 assists in one year. Orr led the league in scoring twice, and won the Hart Trophy as MVP three times. He was a great stickhandler, and his skating skill was unmatched. Sadly, Orr suffered serious injuries in both knees, forcing him to retire in 1978.

September 6, 2008

Slovakia beat Bulgaria 82–0 in a qualifying tournament for women's hockey at the 2010 Vancouver Olympics. It was a record score for a women's game in an event recognized by the International Ice Hockey Federation.

September 7, 1945

Jacques Lemaire was born in LaSalle, Quebec. Lemaire starred for 12 seasons with the Montreal Canadiens, from 1967 to 1979, and helped them win the Stanley Cup eight times.

September 8, 1972

Fans booed Team Canada during a 5–3 loss to the Soviets in Vancouver. Canada had just one win and one tie while playing the first four games of the Summit Series in Canadian cities. The last four games would all be played in Moscow.

September 9, 1997

Mario Lemieux, Bryan Trottier and Glen Sather were all named to the Hockey Hall of Fame. Three years later, Lemieux made a comeback with the Pittsburgh Penguins. He joined Gordie Howe and Guy Lafleur as the third player in history to return to the NHL after being elected to the Hall of Fame.

September 10, 1966

Joe Nieuwendyk was born in Oshawa, Ontario. He played 20 seasons in the NHL with five different teams and scored 564 goals.

September 11, 1987

Wayne Gretzky set up Mario Lemieux for the winning goal in overtime as Team Canada beat the Soviet Union 6–5 in the final game to win the Canada Cup.

September 17, 1985
Alex Ovechkin was born in Moscow. He played for Dynamo
Moscow in Russia before making his NHL debut in 2005–06.
Ovechkin played in the top league in Russia when he was only
16 years old.

September 18, 1933
Scotty Bowman was born in Montreal. Bowman coached for
30 seasons in the NHL with five different teams.

September 19, 1992

Eric Lindros made his NHL debut with Philadelphia in a preseason exhibition game against the Quebec Nordiques.

September 20, 1939

The NHL announced that it would carry on "in a manner as close to normal as possible" following the start of World War II. Later, so many NHL players joined the armed forces there was talk the league might have to shut down. It never did.

September 21, 1955

Matti Hagman was born in Helsinki, Finland. Hagman was the first player who was born and raised in Finland to play in the NHL. His son Niklas Hagman joined the NHL in 2001–02.

September 22, 1934

The NHL added the penalty shot to its rule book. Initially, the shot had to be taken from within a 10-foot circle drawn on the ice 11.5 metres (38 feet) in front of the net.

September 23, 1979

Wayne Gretzky and the Edmonton Oilers played their first NHL game. It was a preseason exhibition game in Brandon, Manitoba.

September 24, 1957

The Montreal Canadiens (and the Montreal Forum) were sold to Senator Hartland Molson and his brother, Thomas H.P. Molson. The Molson family owned the Canadiens until 1972.

The Big E

Players who stand 6'4" and weigh over 200 pounds aren't unusual in the NHL today. But they were when Eric Lindros was making his mark. His size, speed and skill had people calling him "The Next One" . . . as in the next great NHL superstar after Wayne Gretzky and Mario Lemieux.

The Quebec Nordiques had the first pick in the 1991 NHL Draft. But the Lindros family told Quebec that Lindros didn't want to play for them. They picked him anyway, and Lindros refused to report to the team.

While he waited to see what Quebec would do, Lindros played with Team Canada at the 1991 Canada Cup, the 1992 World Junior Championship and the 1992 Winter Olympics. Finally, just before the 1992 NHL Draft, the Nordiques traded Lindros. However, both the Flyers and the Rangers believed they had made a deal for him. In the end, Lindros went to Philadelphia. Quebec got six players, two draft picks, and $15 million.

In the early years of his career, Lindros was one of the best players in the NHL. However, he suffered many injuries and was never fully able to live up to the hype.

September 25, 1926

The NHL officially granted new franchises to Detroit and Chicago. Detroit's team was originally called the Cougars. They played their first season in Windsor, Ontario, in 1926–27 because the new arena being built in Detroit wasn't ready.

September 26, 1972

After falling behind three games to one (with one tie) Team Canada rallied for its second straight win to even up the Summit Series with the Soviet Union.

September 27, 1983

Jay Bouwmeester was born in Edmonton, Alberta. In 1999–2000, he was the youngest Canadian player ever to play at the World Junior Championships. Bouwmeester was only 16 years and three months old.

September 28, 1972

Paul Henderson scored with 34 seconds left in the game to give Team Canada a 6–5 win over the Soviet Union. Canada won the eight-game series four games to three with one tie. Henderson scored the winning goal in each of the last three games.

September 29, 2007

Anaheim and Los Angeles opened the 2007–08 NHL season in London, England. The Kings won the game 4–1, but the Ducks bounced back with a 4–1 win of their own the very next day.

September 30, 2008

The New York Rangers beat SC Bern 8–1 in a preseason exhibition game in Switzerland. This was the first time that a Swiss team ever faced an NHL team.

Henderson was Our Hero

From 1920 until 1961, Canadian teams dominated international hockey tournaments. Then the Soviet Union took over. International hockey was only for amateur players, but fans were sure the best NHL pros could trounce the Soviets. So a series was created in 1972 to let NHL stars face the best Soviet players.

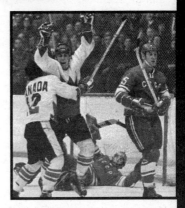

When the Summit Series started on September 2, Team Canada scored just 30 seconds after the opening face-off. Things looked good. But the Soviets bounced back for a 7–3 victory. After four games at home, Team Canada had only one win and one tie. Canadian fans even booed their team in Vancouver after a 5–3 loss.

The rest of the games were played in the Soviet Union. After a 5–4 loss in the first game in Moscow, Team Canada won two straight to even the series. Canadians were pumped for Game 8. Businesses stopped. Schools brought in televisions. The country was at a standstill. When Team Canada fell behind 5–3, it looked bad. But they tied it up in the third period. Then Paul Henderson scored the winning goal and Canadians went crazy! Ask anyone who was alive at the time, and they'll probably be able to tell you exactly where they were when Henderson scored.

October 1, 2008
The New York Rangers beat Russia's Metallurg Magnitogorsk 4–3 at a game in Berne, Switzerland, in the first game played for the Victoria Cup. The Victoria Cup was created in 2007 to pit NHL teams against top teams from Europe.

October 2, 1999
Boston's Ray Bourque scored his 386th career goal, making him the highest-scoring defenseman in NHL history.

October 3, 1997
The first NHL regular-season game to be played outside of North America took place in Tokyo, Japan. Vancouver beat Anaheim 3-2.

October 4, 2008
The NHL opened the 2008–09 season with two games in Europe. The Rangers beat Tampa Bay 2–1 in Prague and Pittsburgh beat Ottawa 4–3 in Stockholm.

October 5, 2005
For the first time in NHL history, all 30 teams were in action on the same night. The opening night of the 2005–06 season was important for another reason too. Both Sidney Crosby and Alex Ovechkin made their NHL debuts.

October 6, 2001
An outdoor hockey game was played in the football stadium at Michigan State University, where Michigan State tied the University of Michigan 3–3. The crowd of 74,544 set an all-time record for a hockey game.

October 7, 1959
Future Hall of Famer Stan Mikita scored the first goal of his NHL career. Mikita was born in Czechoslovakia, but grew up in Canada. On the same day in 1990, Jaromir Jagr — another Czechoslovakian — scored his first NHL goal.

Take It Outside

Hockey began in the great outdoors, played on frozen lakes and rivers. Even though hockey moved inside in 1875, many people still learn to play on outdoor rinks. And the NHL has been going back to hockey's roots with

Wayne Gretzky and Guy Carbonneau at the Heritage Classic

its own outdoor games.

The success of the outdoor game at Michigan State in 2001 inspired the NHL to stage its first outdoor game too. "The Heritage Classic" was held at Edmonton's Commonwealth Stadium on November 22, 2003. The temperature was a frosty –18° Celsius, yet a crowd of 57,167 filled the seats. The Oilers beat the Canadiens 2–0 in an old-timers game in the afternoon, but Montreal beat Edmonton 4–3 in the NHL game that followed.

The NHL held its next outdoor game in 2008, when Buffalo hosted Pittsburgh at Ralph Wilson Stadium. The temperature was higher, but it snowed during the game. The crowd of 71,217 saw the Penguins beat the Sabres 2–1 in a shootout. Sidney Crosby scored the winning goal. The "Winter Classic" is sure to continue in the years to come.

October 8, 1953

Earl "Dutch" Reibel set an NHL record by getting four assists in his very first game. Reibel led the New York Rangers to a 4–1 win over Detroit.

October 9, 1952

Danny Gallivan made his first broadcast as the regular play-by-play voice of the Montreal Canadiens on radio. The next year he began calling games from Montreal for *Hockey Night in Canada* on television.

October 10, 1987

Doug Jarvis of the Hartford Whalers played his 964th consecutive game, having never missed a game since breaking into the NHL with the Montreal Canadiens in 1975. His NHL-record "ironman" streak finally ended when he sat out the very next night. He never played another game in the NHL after that.

October 11, 1952

The CBC broadcast the very first televised *Hockey Night in Canada*. Rene Lecavalier called the play-by-play in French. Foster Hewitt called the first TV game from Toronto on November 1, 1952.

October 12, 2000

Goalie Manny Legace recorded his first career shutout, leading Detroit to a 4–0 win over Chicago.

October 13, 1947

The NHL played its first official All-Star Game after staging three special All-Star benefit games during the 1930s. A team of All-Stars beat the Stanley Cup champion Toronto Maple Leafs 4–3. From 1947 to 1965, the All-Star Game was always held before the start of the season. Since 1967, it's been held in the middle of the season.

All-Star Honours

The idea of picking hockey's top players is almost as old as the game itself. As early as the 1890s, sportswriters published personal lists of All-Star players in their newspaper columns. The first big hockey All-Star Game

Alex Ovechkin hams it up during the 2009 All-Star Weekend

was played on January 2, 1908. The game was held to raise money for the family of Hod Stuart, a top player who had drowned during the summer of 1907.

The NHL staged three All-Star Games during the 1930s. These games were all played to raise money for the families of players who had been killed or injured.

In 1946 a reporter from Chicago wanted to stage a game between the Stanley Cup champions and a team of NHL All-Stars. Money raised by the game would go toward local charities and a players' emergency fund. In 1947 the first official NHL All-Star Game was played in Toronto.

Except for two years in the 1950s, the All-Star Game would match the Stanley Cup champions against the All-Stars. Since 1968 the game has usually matched All-Stars from one NHL conference against All-Stars from the other. Gordie Howe is the oldest player to play in the All-Star Game at 51. Steve Yzerman is the youngest player at 18.

October 14, 1979
Wayne Gretzky scored his first NHL goal. It was a power-play goal with 69 seconds left in the game to give Edmonton a 4–4 tie with Vancouver. Gretzky actually fanned on his backhand shot, but the puck dribbled between the legs of goalie Glen Hanlon.

October 15, 1989
Wayne Gretzky passed Gordie Howe to become the NHL's all-time scoring leader. Gretzky got an assist early in the game to tie Howe with 1,850 points, then tied the game in the third period. He scored in overtime to the give the Los Angeles Kings a 5–4 win over his old team, the Edmonton Oilers.

October 16, 1999
Scott Gomez scored his first NHL goal. He also got two assists to lead the New Jersey Devils past the New York Islanders 4–1. Gomez was the first Hispanic player to play in the NHL.

October 17, 1991
Paul Coffey of the Pittsburgh Penguins became the top-scoring defenseman in NHL history after he got two assists in an 8–5 win over the Islanders, giving him 1,053 career points.

October 18, 2008
Pittsburgh's Sidney Crosby and Evgeni Malkin both reached milestones on the same play: Crosby scored his 100th career goal and Malkin got an assist for his 200th career point. Crosby asked for the puck to be split in half so they could each have a souvenir.

October 19, 1957
Montreal Canadiens legend Maurice Richard became the first player in NHL history to score 500 career goals. Richard reached the milestone at home in a 3–1 win over Chicago.

Gretzky and Gordie

Wayne Gretzky was 11 years old when he first met his hero Gordie Howe. It was at a celebrity sports dinner in Gretzky's hometown of Brantford, Ontario, in 1972. This picture of Howe with a hockey stick hooked around Gretzky's neck would become a symbol of the way their lives seemed to be linked.

Gretzky was already a celebrity. In 85 games with his minor hockey team in Brantford that winter, Gretzky had scored 378 goals. Howe had collected 786 goals and 1,809 points in his NHL career at that time. He would later push those totals to 801 goals and 1,850 points in his 26 NHL seasons. People considered Howe's records to be unbreakable. But Gretzky began to pile up points from the moment he entered the NHL in 1979.

In his second NHL season, Gretzky set a new single-season record with 164 points. The next year, he scored 92 goals and had 212 points. Gretzky broke Howe's record early in the 1989–90 season. By the time he retired in 1999, Gretzky had collected 894 goals and 1,963 assists for 2,857 points in the NHL.

October 20, 1993

Two Gretzkys faced each other in an NHL game. Wayne Gretzky had a goal and two assists to lead Los Angeles to a 4–3 win over Brent Gretzky and the Tampa Bay Lightning. Wayne had also faced his brother Keith Gretzky in a preseason exhibition game in 1987.

October 21, 2006

Pittsburgh's Jordan Staal became the youngest player in NHL history to score a goal on a penalty shot. He was 18 years and one month old.

October 22, 1957

Chicago rookie Bobby Hull scored the first goal of his NHL career. Hull got the first goal of the game in a 2–1 win over Boston.

October 23, 2008

Canadian women's team star Kim St. Pierre played goal in practice with the Montreal Canadiens. She filled in for Carey Price, who was sick with the flu.

October 24, 2002

Colorado's Patrick Roy played in his 972nd career game, breaking Terry Sawchuk's record for most games played in the NHL by a goalie. Roy wound up playing 1,029 games in his career.

October 25, 1984

Guy Lafleur scored his 518th and final goal as a member of the Montreal Canadiens. His next goal would come nearly four years later with the New York Rangers.

October 26, 1997

Steve Yzerman of Detroit broke former Red Wing Alex Delvecchio's NHL record for being the longest-serving captain in league history. Delvecchio had been team captain in Detroit for just over 11 seasons. In the end, Yzerman served as captain for 20 seasons.

Flower Power

Guy Lafleur's speed and skill made him the most exciting player in the NHL during the 1970s. Lafleur led the NHL in points three years in a row, from 1975–76 to 1977–78, and topped 50 goals for six straight seasons. He won the Hart Trophy as MVP twice and helped the Canadiens win the Stanley Cup five times.

Lafleur was known as "The Flower," the English translation of his last name. French fans called him "le Demon Blond" (The Blond Demon) because of his blazing speed and long blond hair.

But by the 1980s, Lafleur was slowing down. After 19 games of the 1984–85 season, he had scored just two goals. He decided to retire on November 26, 1984. But around the time he was elected to the Hockey Hall of Fame in 1988, Lafleur announced he was going to make a comeback. He signed with the New York Rangers, and then spent two seasons with the Quebec Nordiques before retiring for good in 1991.

October 27, 1995

The Red Wings made history by playing five Russian players together as a unit during a 3–0 win at Calgary. Viachslav Fetisov, Vladimir Konstantinov, Igor Larionov, Sergei Fedorov and Vyacheslav Kozlov had all been teammates back in Russia, too.

October 28, 1993

The Toronto Maple Leafs became the first team in NHL history to start a season with 10 consecutive wins.

October 29, 2000

New Jersey's John Madden and Randy McKay each scored four goals in a 9–0 win over Pittsburgh. Madden and McKay became the first NHL teammates to do that since January 14, 1922, when brothers Sprague and Odie Cleghorn each scored four goals to lead the Canadiens past the Hamilton Tigers 10–6.

October 30, 2008

Tampa Bay rookie Steven Stamkos scored his first NHL goal. In fact, he scored two in a 5–2 win over Buffalo.

October 31, 1942

For the first time in NHL history, the regular season began in October. Two games were on the schedule. The Canadiens beat the Bruins 3–2 and the Leafs beat the Rangers 7–2. In earlier years, the NHL season had always started in November or even December.

November 1, 1959

Montreal Canadiens goalie Jacques Plante wore a mask in a game for the first time. Plante was not the first to wear a mask, but he was the first one to make them popular. (See February 20, 1930)

November 2, 1947

In one of the biggest trades in hockey history, Chicago sent two-time NHL scoring champion Max Bentley to Toronto. The Maple Leafs also got one other player. They gave up five players in return, including the complete forward line of Gus Bodnar, Bud Poile and Gaye Stewart.

Saving Face

By the start of the 1959–60 season, Jacques Plante had a long list of injuries. He had fractured each of his cheekbones once and broken his nose twice. He'd also had about 150 stitches to fix up all the cuts on his face. For a goalie in

those days, this was nothing unusual.

Jacques Plante was not like other goalies. He was one of the first to roam from his crease to get loose pucks. He stopped dump-ins behind the net, and sometimes raced out almost to the blue line to pass the puck to his defensemen. Then, after having surgery on his nose during the 1957–58 season, Plante started wearing a mask in practice. It was too big and bulky to wear in a game, but by the fall of 1959 Plante had a mask that was light, tight and unbreakable.

Canadiens coach Toe Blake didn't want Plante to wear his mask in games. So Plante didn't wear it — until the night of November 1, 1959. A shot from the Rangers' Andy Bathgate hit Plante right in the face. It cut him open from his nostrils to his lip. When Plante returned to the net, he was wearing his mask. Soon goalies everywhere were wearing them too.

November 3, 1978

One day after being traded by the Indianapolis Racers, Wayne Gretzky played his first game for the Edmonton Oilers while they were part of the World Hockey Association. He wore number 20 because the Oilers didn't have a 99 sweater ready yet. Gretzky played his first NHL game with the Oilers on October 10, 1979.

November 4, 1962

Detroit's Bill Gadsby became the first defenseman in NHL history to record 500 career points. Gadsby reached the milestone with an assist on a goal by Parker MacDonald.

November 5, 1955

Jean Béliveau of the Montreal Canadiens scored three goals in 44 seconds. All three goals were scored while Boston's Hal Laycoe was in the penalty box. After the season, the NHL changed the rules so that a player serving a two-minute penalty would come back on the ice if the other team scored a power-play goal.

November 6, 1990

Dominik Hasek played his first NHL game, a 1-1 tie between Chicago and the Harford Whalers. Hasek was just a backup with the Blackhawks, but became a star after being traded to Buffalo in 1992.

November 7, 1968

Red Berenson scored six goals to lead St. Louis to an 8–0 win over the Flyers in Philadelphia. Seven players in NHL history have scored six goals in a game, but Berenson is the only one to do it while playing on the road.

November 8, 1952

Maurice Richard scored the 325th goal of his career. At the time, Richard broke Nels Stewart's all-time NHL record of 324 goals. Richard had scored his very first goal on the exact same day back in 1942.

Rocketing Into Their Hearts

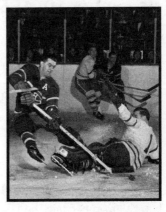

Maurice Richard was a natural goal-scorer. Even as a boy, his talent was obvious. But Richard got hurt a lot. While still playing amateur hockey, he missed one full season with a broken left leg, and most of another with a broken wrist. As a rookie with the Montreal Canadiens in 1942–43, Richard broke his right leg after just 16 games. He worried that he was already through as a hockey player . . . but he was just getting started.

Finally healthy in 1943–44, Richard scored 32 goals to rank among the leaders. He also helped the Canadiens win the Stanley Cup. Richard wasn't the fastest skater, but he was powerful and very intense and could really fire the puck. He became known as "The Rocket."

During the 1944–45 season, Richard scored 50 goals in 50 games. But being hockey's greatest goal-scorer meant that everyone was after him. For fighting through it all — even though his own temper often got the better of him — Richard became more than just a hockey player. He became a hero to French Canadians who were trying to get ahead in an English-speaking world.

November 9, 1984

The Edmonton Oilers beat Washington 8–5 to go 15 games in a row without a loss since the start of the season, with 12 wins and three ties. The old record of 14 was set by the Montreal Canadiens in 1943–44.

November 10, 1963

Gordie Howe scored his 545th career goal to move past Maurice Richard into first place on the NHL's all-time goal-scoring list. Howe went on to score 801 goals in his career. (See March 23, 1994)

November 11, 1930

The NHL played its first game in Philadelphia. The New York Rangers beat the Philadelphia Quakers 3–0. After a horrible season, they dropped out of the league. The NHL did not return to Philadelphia until expansion in 1967.

November 12, 1942

Bep Guidolin became the youngest player in league history making his NHL debut for Boston at just 16 years and 11 months. The Bruins added Guidolin to their lineup because so many NHL players were serving in the military during World War II.

November 13, 1984

Bernie Nicholls became the first player in NHL history to score a goal in all four periods of a game. He scored in the first, second, third and overtime to lead Los Angeles to a 5–4 win over the Quebec Nordiques.

November 14, 1998

Brett Hull of the Dallas Stars picked up an assist for the 1,000th point of his career. Of more than 100 fathers and sons to play in the NHL, Brett and Bobby Hull are the only ones who have both reached this milestone.

November 15, 1973

Bobby Orr had three goals and four assists to lead the Bruins past the Rangers 10–2. At the time, Orr's seven points in one game set a record for defensemen.

November 16, 1926

Eddie Shore played his first game in the NHL with the Boston Bruins. There was no Norris Trophy for the best defenseman back in Shore's day, but he won the Hart Trophy as league MVP four times.

November 17, 2007

New Jersey's Martin Brodeur won the 500th game of his NHL career. Brodeur was just the second goalie in NHL history to win 500 games. Patrick Roy had been the first.

November 18, 2002

Canadiens captain Saku Koivu scored his first career hat trick. Koivu's three goals helped the Canadiens beat Pittsburgh 5–4 in overtime.

November 19, 2007

Jaromir Jagr scored his 600th career goal. Jagr was the second New York Rangers player to reach the milestone within just a few weeks. Teammate Brendan Shanahan had scored his 600th goal on October 5, 2007.

November 20, 1934

Toronto's Harvey "Busher" Jackson became the first player in NHL history to score four goals in a single period. His four goals in the third led the Maple Leafs past the St. Louis Eagles 5–2.

Myles From Shore

Eddie Shore worked on the family farm in Saskatchewan. When he had time for sports, he usually played soccer or baseball. He didn't start playing hockey seriously until he was a teenager. But by the time he was 22, he was good enough to play professionally.

Shore started as a forward. He moved back to defense in 1925–26 when he played for the Edmonton Eskimos in the old Western Hockey League. When the WHL collapsed, the NHL snapped up all its best players and Shore was signed by the Boston Bruins. The Bruins had been one of the NHL's worst teams. But in Shore's first season with the team, they reached the Stanley Cup Finals and won it in his third year.

Shore was the NHL's best offensive defenseman. He was also one of the league's toughest players. Often, in his end-to-end rushes, instead of deking around his opponents, he'd just knock them over.

The New York Rangers once tried to get Shore from the Bruins. They offered Boston a rookie defenseman named Myles Lane. Bruins boss Art Ross turned them down, saying, "You're so many Myles from Shore, you need a life preserver!"

November 21, 1942

The NHL decided to stop using overtime for regular-season games. With wartime restrictions on train travel, overtime sometimes made it hard for teams to catch their train after a game. The NHL didn't bring overtime back for the regular season until 1983.

November 22, 1986

Edmonton's Wayne Gretzky scored his 500th career goal. Gretzky reached the milestone in just his 575th game. No one in NHL history has ever scored 500 goals so quickly.

November 23, 1944

Because of injuries and players serving in the military during World War II, the Toronto Maple Leafs could only dress 11 players for their game in Boston. The Bruins beat Toronto 5–1.

November 24, 1979

Los Angeles Kings star Charlie Simmer scored the first goal in a 13-game goal-scoring streak. Simmer fell three games short of the all-time record, but his streak was the longest in modern hockey history. (See February 15, 1922)

November 25, 1951

Black Hawks trainer Moe Roberts had to play the third period after goalie Harry Lumley got hurt. Just a few weeks shy of his 46th birthday, Roberts became the oldest player in NHL history at the time. He had been a goalie during his 20-year career but hadn't played a game in the NHL since the 1933–34 season!

Overtime Over Time

The rules for overtime in the regular season have changed a lot during the history of the NHL. When the league began in the 1917–18 season, any game that was tied after 60 minutes would continue into

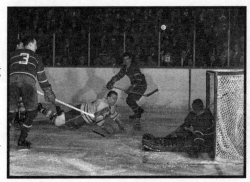

Bill Barilko scores the overtime goal that won the Leafs the Cup in 1951

overtime for however long it took a team to finally score the winning goal . . . just like in the playoffs. That remained the rule until the end of the 1920–21 season.

Beginning in 1921–22, the NHL limited overtime to just one 20-minute period. This was the rule until the end of the 1926–27 season. In 1927–28, the NHL decided the overtime period should only be 10 minutes long.

During the seasons from 1917–18 to 1927–28, overtime was always sudden death. That meant whichever team scored first was the winner. Starting in 1928–29, overtime was played for a full 10 minutes no matter how many goals were scored! If both teams scored, the game ended in a tie. When overtime returned to the regular season in 1983, it became a five-minute, sudden-death period. Then, in the 2005–06 season, the league decided that games would go to shootouts to decide a winner if no one scored in overtime.

November 26, 1961

Detroit's Gordie Howe became the first player in NHL history to play in 1,000 regular-season games. Howe went on to play in the NHL until he was 51 years old.

November 27, 1960

Gordie Howe picked up an assist in a 2–0 win over Toronto. It gave him 1,000 points in his career. Howe was the first player in NHL history to reach this milestone. (See October 15, 1989)

November 28, 1979

Billy Smith was the first NHL goalie to be credited with a goal. Smith was the last New York Islanders player to touch the puck before Rob Ramage of the Colorado Rockies scored on his own net!

November 29, 1924

The Canadiens beat the Toronto St. Pats 7–1 in the first game played at the Montreal Forum. The Forum had actually been built for the Montreal Maroons, but the Canadiens got to play there first because there were problems with the ice at their home rink.

Howe About That

Gordie Howe was just 15 years old when he went to his first NHL training camp. He left his home in Saskatoon to go to Winnipeg, where the New York Rangers were working out. Howe had a terrible time. He left camp early and returned to the family farm. The Rangers didn't sign him.

A year later, Howe was invited to work out with the Detroit Red Wings. He made a much better impression. Detroit signed him, and he made it to the NHL as an 18-year-old in 1946–47.

Howe had an effortless skating style. He was fast and strong. He could also shoot the puck equally well left-handed or right-handed. Howe was teamed with veterans Sid Abel and Ted Lindsay. They were soon dubbed "The Production Line" because of all the points they produced. In 1950–51 Howe led the league in scoring for the first of four years in a row.

When Howe's games in the NHL are combined with his games in the World Hockey Association, he played a total of 2,186 games before he retired for good in 1980.

November 30, 2005

The San Jose Sharks got Joe Thornton from Boston in a trade for three players. Thornton went on to win the Art Ross Trophy for the 2005–06 season. He is the only player in history to be traded during a season in which he won the NHL scoring title.

December 1, 1924

The Boston Bruins beat the Montreal Maroons 2–1 in the first NHL game to be played in the United States. The Bruins and the Maroons were both new teams in the NHL for the 1924–25 season. Boston was the first American NHL team.

December 2, 1989

Mario Lemieux scored three goals and picked up an assist to lead the Penguins to a 7–4 win over the Quebec Nordiques. Lemieux's third goal was the 316th of his NHL career, tying him with Jean Pronovost as the Penguins' all-time leading goal scorer. Lemieux went on to score 690 goals in his career, all of them with the Penguins.

December 3, 1929

The Boston Bruins beat the Montreal Canadiens 3–1. It was the first of 14 wins in a row for the Bruins. That's still a team record. It was also the first of 20 straight wins at home . . . which is still an NHL record.

December 4, 1909

The Montreal Canadiens were founded at a meeting of the National Hockey Association. The NHA became the NHL in 1917. Today, the Canadiens are the oldest team in professional hockey. They have won the Stanley Cup more than anyone else.

Super Mario

Bobby Orr called Mario Lemieux the most skilled player he had ever seen. Coming from Orr, it was high praise. But like Bobby Orr, Mario Lemieux's career was plagued by injuries, and even illness. He suffered from severe back pains and from a battle with Hodgkin's disease, a form of cancer. Yet Lemieux was one of the greatest players in hockey history.

Lemieux was Pittsburgh's first choice in the 1984 NHL Entry Draft. The Penguins were struggling, but Lemieux quickly became the best player in the NHL, and Pittsburgh became the best team in the league. He led them to the Stanley Cup in 1991 and 1992.

Lemieux was big, but he didn't throw his weight around. He beat players with speed and dekes. He led the NHL in scoring six times in his career. Only Wayne Gretzky has won more scoring titles.

Injuries forced Lemieux to retire in 1997. In 1999 he organized a group that bought the Penguins. When he made a comeback in 2000, Lemieux became the first player in NHL history to play for a team that he also owned! He retired for good in 2006.

December 5, 1968

Goalie Tony Esposito made his first NHL start. He gave up two goals in a 2–2 tie with the Boston Bruins — Tony's brother, Phil Esposito, scored both goals against him! (See June 11, 1969)

December 6, 1990

The NHL announced that two new expansion teams would join the league. The Ottawa Senators and Tampa Bay would begin play in 1992–93.

December 7, 1977
Gordie Howe scored his 1,000th career goal in major professional hockey. In the end, he finished his career with 1,072 goals. He is only one of three players to have reached 1,000 goals, along with Wayne Gretzky and Bobby Hull.

December 8, 1987
Flyers goalie Ron Hextall fired the puck the length of the ice to score a goal on Boston's empty net. Hextall was the first goalie in NHL history to shoot and score.

December 9, 1992
Boston's Gordie Roberts became the first American-born player to play in 1,000 games in the NHL.

December 10, 1983
The Buffalo Sabres beat the Bruins 4–2 in Boston. The Sabres went on to win 10 in a row on the road, which was a record at the time. The Detroit Red Wings broke that record with 12 straight road wins in 2005–06.

December 11, 1985
Wayne Gretzky tied an NHL record with seven assists in one game. He led Edmonton past Chicago 12–9. The 21 goals scored in that game tied an NHL record set way back on January 10, 1920 when the Montreal Canadiens beat the Toronto St. Pats 14–7.

December 12, 1953
Montreal's Maurice Richard moved into first place on the NHL's all-time scoring list. Richard picked up a goal and two assists in a 7–2 win over the New York Rangers to give him 611 points in his career.

December 13, 1995

Detroit's Paul Coffey became the fourth player in NHL history to get 1,000 career assists. He was the first defenseman to reach the milestone.

December 14, 1982

Marcel Dionne of the Los Angeles Kings scored the 500th goal of his career. He was the ninth player in NHL history to reach the 500-goal plateau.

December 15, 1995

Deron Quint tied the NHL record for the two fastest goals in a game when he scored just four seconds apart. He scored at 7:51 and 7:55 of the second period to lead the Winnipeg Jets past Edmonton 9–4. (See January 3, 1931)

December 16, 1950

Two future Hall of Famers made their NHL debuts for the Montreal Canadiens in the same game. Jean Béliveau and Bernie Geoffrion both played in a 1–1 tie with the New York Rangers.

December 17, 1924

Goalies Jake Forbes of the Hamilton Tigers and Alec Connell of the Ottawa Senators played in the first 0–0 tie in NHL history. It was the first scoreless game in eight seasons of NHL action.

December 18, 1983

Wayne Gretzky had two goals and two assists to lead Edmonton past Winnipeg 7–5. The four points gave Gretzky 100 for the season in just 34 games. No one in NHL history has reached the 100-point mark faster.

Coffey Talk

Paul Coffey may have been the best skater in hockey history. He was blazing fast and super smooth.

Coffey worked hard to become a great skater, but a lot of his skill was just natural-born talent. He did have one trick, though. He used to wear skates that were too small. He once joked to a reporter that he wanted to fool his feet into thinking that the faster they skated, the faster the game would end and he could take the skates off.

Coffey's blazing speed made him a perfect fit with Wayne Gretzky and the high-flying Edmonton Oilers. He joined the team in 1980, and was soon being compared to Bobby Orr. During the 1983–84 season, Coffey joined Orr as just the second defenseman in NHL history to score 40 goals in a single season. Two years later, Coffey nearly became the only defenseman in history to score 50 goals in one season. He wound up with 48, breaking Orr's old record of 46.

Even after he left the Oilers, Coffey was often among the league's leaders in assists. When he retired in 2001, his lifetime total of 1,135 assists ranked fourth in NHL history.

December 19, 1917

The first season in NHL history got underway. Two games were on the schedule that night. The Montreal Canadiens beat the Ottawa Senators 7–4 in one game. The Montreal Wanderers beat the Toronto Arenas 10–9 in the other.

December 20, 2007

Marian Gaborik had five goals and one assist to lead the Minnesota Wild to a 6–3 win over the New York Rangers. Gaborik was the first NHL player in 11 years to score five goals in one game.

December 21, 1937

Chicago's Paul Thompson blasted a shot past Boston's Tiny Thompson. It was the first time in NHL history that a player had scored a goal against his brother. Paul's goal broke Tiny's shutout, but the Bruins still beat the Black Hawks 2–1.

December 22, 1976

The first official World Junior Championship tournament began. It ended on January 2, 1977. The Soviet Union beat Canada 6–4 in the final game to win the gold medal. Canada got the silver. Czechoslovakia took the bronze.

December 23, 1978

Bryan Trottier set an NHL record with six points in a single period. He had three goals and three assists in the second period to lead the Islanders past the Rangers 9–4.

December 24, 1972

The Los Angeles Kings beat the Oakland Seals 5–3 in the last NHL game ever played on Christmas Eve. Serge Bernier scored four goals for Los Angeles. Earlier that evening, Chicago beat Toronto 5–1 and the Rangers beat Detroit 5–0. Since 1973, the NHL has always had a break in the schedule for Christmas Eve and Christmas Day.

Phantom Joe

Hockey was a very different game when the NHL began. The only way to advance the puck was by skating with it and stickhandling. Forward passing was against the rules. The six men who started the game often played the full 60 minutes. Seasons were also much shorter, but since so few players got to play, the best ones scored plenty of goals.

Joe Malone was probably the best stickhandler in hockey when the NHL began. He was known as "Phantom Joe" because of his slick moves on the ice. It was as if he could disappear and reappear . . . like some kind of a ghost. On the first night in NHL history, Malone scored five goals for the Montreal Canadiens. He went on to lead the league with 44 goals during the 1917–18 season. He did it in just 20 games!

Malone's 44 goals remained an NHL record for 23 years. Today, the NHL record for goals in one season is 92. Still, no one has ever beaten Malone's scoring average of 2.2 goals per game. These days, a player would have to score 180 goals in 82 games to equal Malone's pace.

December 25, 1970
Toronto's Norm Ullman scored twice to become the seventh player in NHL history to reach 400 career goals.

December 26, 1925
The New York Americans and Pittsburgh Pirates combined to set an NHL record for the most shots on goal by both teams in one game. New York outshot Pittsburgh 73–68 for a total of 141 shots. The Americans won the game 3–1.

December 27, 1999
Rookie Roberto Luongo stopped 34 shots for his first career shutout. The New York Islanders beat Boston 3–0.

December 28, 2004
At 16 years and four months old, Sidney Crosby became the youngest player to score a goal at the World Junior Championship. Team Canada beat Switzerland 7–2 that day, and went on to win the gold medal. (See January 4, 2005)

December 29, 1955
NHL referees and linesmen wore black and white striped shirts in a game for the first time. The game was in Montreal, and the Canadiens beat the Leafs 5–2. Previously, referees had worn sweaters that looked too much like the hockey players'.

December 30, 1981
Wayne Gretzky scored five goals to lead Edmonton past Philadelphia 7–5. The five goals gave Gretzky 50 for the season in just 39 games. No other player in NHL history has ever scored 50 goals so quickly.

December 31, 1988
Mario Lemieux had five goals and three assists to lead Pittsburgh past New Jersey 8–6. All five of Lemieux's goals were scored differently. He scored one at even strength, one on the power-play, one shorthanded, one on a penalty shot and one into an empty net.

Louie Louie

Even though Roberto Luongo played both soccer and hockey until he was 14, he used to write "NHL player" whenever teachers asked him what he wanted to be when he grew up.

In 1997 the New York Islanders picked Luongo fourth overall in the NHL Entry Draft. At that time, no goalie had ever been picked higher since the draft took its current form in 1969. He made his NHL debut with the Islanders on November 28, 1999 and made 43 saves in his very first game. Luongo was traded to Florida after the 1999–2000 season. He spent the next five seasons with the Panthers and, though the team always struggled, Luongo became a star. During the 2003–04 season, he faced more shots (2,475) and made more saves (2,303) than any goalie in NHL history.

Since joining the Vancouver Canucks in 2006, "Louie" has continued to rank among the best — and the busiest — goalies in the NHL.

Eric Zweig

By the age of 10, Eric Zweig was already a budding sports fanatic who was filling his school books with game reports instead of current events. He has been writing professionally about sports and sports history since graduating from Trent University in 1985. His articles have appeared in many Canadian publications including the *Toronto Star*, *The Globe and Mail*, the *Toronto Sun*, the *Ottawa Citizen*, the *Calgary Herald* and *The Beaver*. He has also been a writer/producer with CBC Radio Sports and TSN SportsRadio.

Eric has written several books, including *Hockey Night in the Dominion of Canada*; *Hockey Trivia for Kids*; *A Century of Hockey Heroes, Goals, and Saves*; *Long Shot* and *Star Power*. Eric works as a managing editor at Dan Diamond and Associates and edits the *NHL Official Guide & Record Book*, as well as several other titles.

Eric is a member of the Society for International Hockey Research and the Society for American Baseball Research. He is married and lives in Owen Sound, Ontario, with his wife Barbara, who is also a writer and editor. A former member of the Toronto Blue Jays grounds crew, he still has a champagne bottle from the club's first American League East Division title celebration in 1985.

Photo Credits

Bob Nystrom's overtime goal in 1980 gave the New York Islanders their first of four Stanley Cup Championships. After they won, teammate Clark Gillies let his dog eat out of the Stanley Cup bowl. When asked to explain, Gillies simply said, "Hey, he's a nice dog."

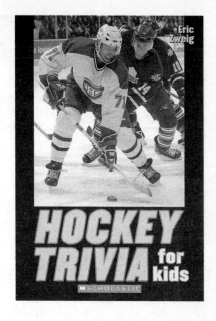

How many pucks does it take to get through an average NHL game? Who was *really* the first goalie to wear a mask? What was the Stanley Cup doing at the bottom of Mario Lemieux's pool?

Find the answer to these questions and more in *Hockey Trivia for Kids!*

Before he reached the NHL, Denis Savard was already part of a famous line with the Montreal Junior Canadiens. Savard centred Denis Cyr and Denis Tremblay on a line known as "Les Trois Denis." Not only did they share a name, they had all been born on the same day and they grew up within three blocks of each other in the Montreal suburb of Verdun!

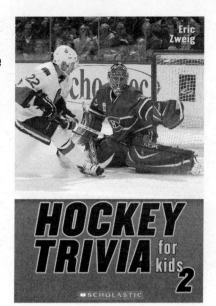

Find out:

- how the Stanley Cup ended up at a road hockey rematch

- what Hall of Famer played all six positions in a single game

- how a player was able score his first NHL goal *twice*

. . . and even more fun and interesting facts about the game we all love, in *Hockey Trivia for Kids 2!*